FLAGS OF ALL NATIONS

by

Cleveland H. Smith
and
Gertrude R. Taylor

THOMAS Y. CROWELL COMPANY
NEW YORK

DEDICATED TO

All the Nations of the World

with the hope that the time will come when "they shall
beat their swords into plowshares, and their spears into
pruninghooks: nation shall not lift up sword against
nation, neither shall they learn war any more."

CONTENTS

PREFACE

FLAGS ARE the symbols of the unity of people. When nations disappear, either through war or the decline of their culture, or when new nations are born, we witness the end or the birth of a new flag.

This book has been written and illustrated to reveal the origin and meaning of the flags of all nations comprising the community of nations, that is the world, regardless of the status of any nation in the war.

The first part of the book is devoted to the story of our flag, the flag of the United States, with which every American should be familiar. The flags of all other nations are presented in alphabetical order.

1

European Flags Planted in the New World by Explorers

THE FLAG of the United States, the symbol of our nation, has often been called the soul of our nation. Certain it is that the design of the flag is a good indication of the character, the spirit, and the history of the American people. When our forefathers left the Old World behind and began to think about forming a more perfect union, a democracy, they left behind them not only monarchs but also royal arms, ensigns armorial, and other kinds of heraldry that are so closely tied up with royalty. The founding fathers chose wisely the flag that should represent the new nation even as they did the principles that should govern it, for our flag has come to be a symbol of liberty, of equality, of opportunity, of religious and personal freedom to people all over the world. The Stars and Stripes has been a source of inspiration to the nation. Likewise it has been buttressed by our deeds.

Throughout the centuries of discovery and exploration of the American continent, the flags of five nations were planted on its shores. Let us look at these first, for the story of our flag may have its antecedents in one or more of these flags.

About five hundred years before Columbus reached the shores of the New World, Leif Ericsson set sail for Greenland. He was driven out of his course to a new country which he called Vinland, a place that has been described

VIKING FLAG   FLAG OF COLUMBUS

variously as Labrador, Newfoundland, and Nova Scotia. He is supposed to have planted there the banner of the Vikings, a white flag containing a raven with wings spread.

The Norse sagas recount the adventures of Leif Ericsson and his discovery of North America. But as no permanent settlement was made, we may consider the discovery of the New World by Columbus as the first claim to some part of the American continent for a European sovereign. He was also the first to leave the flag of that sovereign flying over a colony in the new country.

When Columbus sailed to find what he believed was a new route to India, he set sail under the flag of the United Kingdoms of Leon and Castile whose rulers were King Ferdinand and Queen Isabella. Ponce de Leon who discovered Florida, Hernando de Soto who penetrated to the Mississippi River, and Coronado who explored much of the country west of the Mississippi River all traveled under the flag of Leon and Castile.

Another explorer, John Cabot, was of Italian extraction but sailed under the flag of England. He reached the shores of America near Cape Breton in 1497, and the flag he planted there was the flag of England, a white field with the red cross of St. George.

Three years later, in 1500, Gaspar de Corte-Real, a Portuguese explorer, reached the shores of Labrador and Newfoundland and laid claim to the land for his monarch. He planted the Portuguese flag of blue and white embroidered

2

CROSS OF ST. GEORGE   FLAG OF FRANCE

with the royal arms. But again, as in the case of Leif Ericsson, no permanent settlement was made and the flag disappeared from the continent.

In 1534, Jacques Cartier, a French explorer, set out on an
expedition to discover a passage to China. He was sailing
in the wrong direction. He landed at Newfoundland, went
on to Labrador, then changed his course. He crossed the
Gulf of the St. Lawrence, stopped at what we now know as
Quebec, and claimed the land for the King of France.

The English navigator Henry Hudson, sailing in the service of the Dutch East India Company, was in command of
the *Half Moon* which reached New York, then called New
Amsterdam, in 1609. He carried the flag of the Netherlands,
with the letters "A.O.C." imposed on the white stripe.
"A.O.C." stood for "Algemeene Ost-Indische Compagnie" or
Dutch East India Company.

The fifth and last flag to find its way to the New World
was the Swedish flag. It was raised in 1638 by the Swedish
colonists who settled on either side of the Delaware River
in what has since been incorporated into the State of New
Jersey.

These five flags, the flags of Spain, England, France, the
Netherlands, and Sweden, all claimed some part of America
for their European sovereigns. As we shall see, the last flag
to come was the first to go, that of New Sweden.

In the meantime, other English colonists arrived. In 1607,
the first colonists, brought over by Captain James Smith, set-

3

DUTCH EAST INDIA CO.   **SWEDISH SETTLEMENT'S FLAG**

tled in Virginia. His ship flew the King's colors from the mainmast and the Cross of St. George from the foremast. The Pilgrims, who reached Plymouth Rock in 1620 in the *Mayflower,* also displayed the King's colors from their mainmast and the red cross of St. George from the foremast.

With the expansion of Dutch colonial possessions, the Dutch transferred their interests in the New World to the newly created Dutch West India Company. The New Amsterdam colony replaced the letters "A.O.C." on their flag with "G.W.C." In 1650, the orange stripe in the Netherlands flag was changed to red. Here in New Amsterdam the new red, white, and blue flag made its appearance, too. Five years later, Peter Stuyvesant, governor of New Amsterdam, received orders from Holland to take possession of the Swedish settlement. With a force of about six hundred men he captured the colony of New Sweden for the Dutch. The conquest was short-lived, for in 1664 the English conquered the Dutch and the Netherlands flag vanished from this country. Except for the French and Spanish in the north and south, the English had sovereignty over the New World. The entire coast from Maine to Georgia belonged to them, with ten times as many people in that territory as there were in all the rest of the country. There were many boundary disputes between the French and English. They ended finally in the French and Indian War, which lasted for seven years. At the end of this war, by the Treaty of Paris, France lost her territory in the New World. England received all the land east

DUTCH WEST INDIA CO.

CROSS OF ST. ANDREW

KING'S COLORS

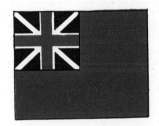

METEOR FLAG

of the Mississippi, including Canada, Newfoundland, and Cape Breton Island. Spain acquired Louisiana and land west of the Mississippi from France. In return for Cuba, she gave England Florida. This left only Spain to rival England in the New World, and though territorially Spain's sphere seems large, it is to be remembered that much of the land she claimed was not populated.

Two British flags have been referred to: the Cross of St. George and the King's colors. As the British flag was to predominate in this country in Revolutionary times, let us take a moment to examine some facts about it. From the thirteenth century until 1606, the British flag was the Cross of St. George. In 1606, the kingdoms of England and Scotland were united under King James I, who decreed the British flag should henceforth be the union of the red cross of St. George with the white cross of St. Andrew. This flag was known as the King's colors. It flew from the masts of the ships bearing the colonists to Jamestown and to Plymouth Rock.

In 1707, England, Scotland, and Wales were united. A Union flag of red, with the crosses of St. George and St. Andrew conjoined in the canton, was established. This flag, frequently called the Meteor flag, was flown by the English colonists both on land and sea until they broke with the mother country.

Colonial and Battle Flags Used
by the Colonists

In ADDITION to the national flags that made their appearance in the New World and the British flags that were used by the English colonists, there were others that preceded the Stars and Stripes. The colonies designed flags, sometimes with the approval of the British government, that were equivalent to our state flags. Since there were threats not only from the Indians, but also from the Dutch, the French on the north, and even from the mother country, the early settlers had to defend their land. The colonies organized militia, each of which had its own flag.

In addition to the colonial and battleflags there were the flags of the Revolutionary period. Among the colonial flags which began to be used during the eighteenth century by the New England colonies, many contained the pine tree motif. The colonists undoubtedly chose the pine tree emblem because it was an emblem that was indigenous to America. It represented to the colonists a design that was meaningful and yet plain and since austerity was a characteristic of the New England colonists, as well it might be in such pioneer days, the plainness of the design made it all the more proper.

The Pine Tree flag used by Washington's six cruisers in 1775, and subsequently by the Massachusetts Navy in almost identical form, consisted of a white field with a pine tree in the center and the motto "An Appeal to Heaven." One of the Revolutionary flags, the flag of Bunker Hill, was blue. The red cross of St. George occupied the canton. In the uppermost corner of the cross there was a pine tree. Another flag known as the Liberty Tree Flag of 1776 bore a pine tree and the words "Liberty Tree—An Appeal to God." The flag of the Massachusetts Navy was white. Its center bore a pine tree round whose trunk a snake was coiled. Above the design were the words "An Appeal to God" and below "Don't Tread on Me."

Another group of flags having the same motif is the rattlesnake group. The rattlesnake design was favored particularly by the Southern colonies. Many lengthy articles have been written on why the rattlesnake emblem was used but we need to go no deeper into the question than to survey the sentiments of the people at that time. The colonists were very intense in their feelings against what they considered injustices in the mother country's governing of them. Such feeling prompted them to pick an emblem which would show their resentment. The rattlesnake seemed appropriate. It is not a design which the colonists would have approved as a national emblem to represent them to the world but they were not yet a nation. When the time came to choose a national flag, their considered judgment of a design was one worthy of a nation. Benjamin Franklin is credited with having suggested the rattlesnake design. The flag of the Virginia colony was white or yellow and had a coiled rattlesnake in the center and underneath the motto "Don't Tread on Me." The First Navy Jack of 1775 was striped alternately red and white. Across the stripes stretched a rattlesnake under which was the motto "Don't Tread on Me." The flag of the Culpepper Minute Men was white. It had a rattlesnake in the center—above, the words "Liberty or Death," below, the familiar slogan "Don't Tread on Me."

WASHINGTON'S CRUISERS

BUNKER HILL FLAG

MASSACHUSETTS NAVY

VIRGINIA COLONY

FIRST NAVY JACK

Plate 1

9

CULPEPPER FLAG

TAUNTON FLAG

FORT MOULTRIE FLAG

EUTAW STANDARD

BEDFORD FLAG

Plate 2

Oppressive measures of taxation and the Navigation Acts finally caused the colonists to take measures against the mother country. The bond of union between the American colonists and Great Britain steadily grew weaker. The Liberty and Union flag of 1774, the red ensign of England but inscribed with the words "Liberty and Union" across the bottom of the flag, first raised at Taunton, Massachusetts, symbolized the colonists' growing resentment.

In the early years of the Revolution, the flags of certain companies, regiments, brigades, and other military units were prominent. Some were to continue to be cherished even down to our own times. The Bunker Hill flag, mentioned previously because of the pine tree motif in the canton, is among the famous flags of American history.

The Philadelphia Light Horse Troop, that escorted General Washington from Philadelphia to New York when he was on his way to Cambridge to assume command of the Continental Army, had a yellow flag that was fringed and almost square. Its canton, consisting of thirteen blue and silver stripes with a center knot tied with thirteen cords, is supposed to have been the first to recognize the thirteen colonies by thirteen stripes. This banner was presented to the men of the troop by their commander, Captain Abraham Markoe, though he was constrained from fighting with the men because he was a Danish subject. The King of Denmark had issued an order to all his subjects forbidding them to take sides in the war against Great Britain.

The Eutaw standard, a square crimson flag, flew at the Battle of Cowpens and at Eutaw Springs, in the final days of the Revolutionary War. Compared with the other battle flags it has a strange appearance. Colonel William Washington was leader of the Cavalry Troop that carried the flag. Before going into battle, he visited his fiancée, Miss Jane Elliot. As he was leaving, she wished him victory and safekeeping and expressed the hope that the flag of his troops would remain aloft. He thanked her but said he had no flag. She is supposed to have taken a pair of scissors, snipped a square of red tapestry from her chair, and given it to him. The original flag has been preserved. It was given to the Washington Light Infantry of Charleston in 1827 by Mrs. Jane Elliott Washington.

Preserved along with other historic relics in the city of Bedford is the Bedford flag. It has a dark red field on which appear three cannon balls and a hand bearing a sword. The hand emerges from a cloud. The words on the scroll, "Vince Aut Morire," mean "Conquer or die." The Minute Men of Bedford carried this flag at the Battle of Concord. The flag, however, was not new. The original flag had been designed, made, and used many years earlier by the English Three County Troop in King Philip's War.

The flag of Fort Moultrie was the first American Revolutionary War flag used in the South. Its design was suggested to Colonel William Moultrie by the blue uniforms of his men and the crescents they wore on their caps. Colonel Moultrie was ordered to take Fort Johnson, South Carolina. After taking the fort he realized that he did not have a flag to raise over it and it was then that he thought of this design. Word came to Colonel Moultrie that the British planned to take the entrance to Charleston by sea. He built a fort of palmetto logs on Sullivan Island where he might better defend the entrance to the city. The British squadron came in and began to bombard the fort, above which floated the Fort Moultrie flag. The flag was hit by a cannon ball and fell, but one of the men, Sergeant William Jasper, rescued it and placed it back up again. His act served to stiffen the determination and spirit of the men who kept firing their guns steadily. After ten hours the British gave up and sailed away. This flag has been perpetuated in the state flag of South Carolina which consists of a blue field, a white crescent in the upper left hand corner and a white palmetto in the center of the flag.

3

Evolution of the Stars and Stripes

THERE ARE other battle and colonial flags that were designed and used by particular sections or units of men but none of these flags can be considered the direct ancestor of our first national flag. The Grand Union flag, also known as the Cambridge flag because it was raised over General Washington's quarters at Cambridge, is the flag that bears this distinction. It was not brought into being by any federal law or direction, since the colonists had at that time no thought of a definite break with England. They had united to force England to allow them representation in Parliament. When a committee of Congress met to discuss the formation of a Continental Army, its maintenance, support and operation, it is possible that they may also have discussed the matter of a flag. Correspondence, minutes of meetings, and other papers do not, however, reveal that any such discussion took place. It is definitely known that on January 1, 1776, the Grand Union flag was raised over General Washington's headquarters on Prospect Hill near Cambridge. The flag was like the Meteor flag. The thirteen stripes represented the thirteen colonies participating in the Revolution.

The presence of the Union Jack in the flag is an indication that the colonies did not entertain any thought of separating from the mother country. On the day that the flag was raised, a message from the King was received and read in the streets of Boston to the people. British representatives of the King and loyalists who were opposed to resisting England construed the flag to be a symbol of submission on the part of General Washington and his rebel colonies because of the Union Jack in the canton of the flag. The British were soon undeceived when the Continental Army drove the British out of Boston. In July of that year, the Declaration of Independence was read, and the Grand Union flag was raised to represent the United States. But with the colonies committed to a new course of action—complete independence —the Union Jack had to be removed from their flag. The flag that evolved was the flag made by Betsy Ross. This is the flag that is specified in our first Flag Act of June 14, 1777, passed by the Continental Congress.

> "Resolved: That the flag of the United States be thirteen stripes, alternate red and white; that the union be thirteen stars, white in a blue field, representing a new constellation."

By this act the arrangement of the stars was not fixed. In the first flag the thirteen stars were arranged in the form of a circle on the blue canton.

Flags of thirteen stars and thirteen stripes carried by military units differed, though, in the way the stars were arranged. In those days the Continental Congress had neither time nor resources to furnish the Continental troops with flags. General Washington was confronted with innumerable problems, not the least of which was how to pay the men and keep them clothed. The Continental troops were aware that a flag with thirteen red and white stripes and thirteen white stars on a blue field had been approved for the flag of the United States. They made flags for themselves that they thought conformed to the approved flag. The men's desire to raise the new flag over their forts accounts for the variety of flags, fitting the general description and yet unlike the Betsy Ross flag, that were used.

The Guilford Flag, which was carried by the North Caro-

GRAND UNION FLAG

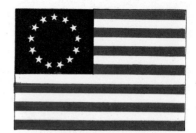

BETSY ROSS FLAG

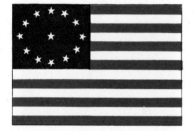

THIRD MARYLAND REGT.
FLAG

BENNINGTON FLAG

FORT Mc HENRY FLAG

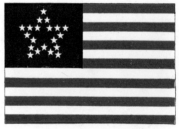

GREAT STAR FLAG

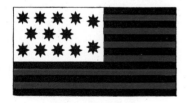

GUILFORD FLAG

FLAG OF 1818

Plate 3

15

lina Militia at the Battle of Guilford in 1781, is much longer and narrower than the Betsy Ross flag: the stripes are red and blue, the canton white with thirteen blue eight-pointed stars arranged in three rows in quincunx order, that is, the stars were placed alternately and not directly under each other.

The flag carried by the Third Maryland Regiment at the Battle of Cowpens in 1781 had thirteen red and white stripes and thirteen white stars in a blue canton. But here, twelve of the stars were arranged in a circle and the thirteenth was in the center of the circle.

The Bennington flag, now in the possession of the Bennington Battle Monument and Historical Association, is another Stars and Stripes flag of unfamiliar pattern. The flag is almost twice as long as it is wide. The white stripes number seven while the red stripes only six. Seven-pointed stars have been used instead of five-pointed stars and the stars are pointed downward rather than upward as in the Betsy Ross flag. Eleven of the stars are arranged in the form of an arch in the canton, the other two are larger than the rest and are placed in the upper corners of the canton.

For eighteen years, the flags continued as prescribed by the first Flag Act. With the admission of two new states to the Union, Vermont in 1791 and Kentucky in 1792, it was proposed that the flag be changed to represent the new states. After considerable debate, the second Flag Act was passed in Congress and approved by President Washington on January 13, 1794. It established:

> "That from and after the first day of May, anno Domini one thousand seven hundred and ninety five, the flag of the United States be fifteen stripes, alternate red and white; that the union be fifteen stars, white on a blue field."

In Tripoli in 1805, the United States Marines raised the flag of fifteen stars and fifteen stripes over their fortifications. The flag that waved over Fort McHenry in September, 1814, and that inspired Francis Scott Key to write the *Star Spangled Banner,* was a flag of this design. Throughout the next twenty-three years, on the high seas and in foreign lands, the flag of the United States was the Stars and Stripes prescribed by the second Flag Act.

Scarcely had the new flag been authorized when another state, Tennessee, was admitted to the Union. Clearly some provision was needed for the entrance of new states to the Union without changing the entire flag. By 1816, Ohio, Louisiana, and Indiana were admitted. In that year, the Honorable Peter H. Wendover, representative from New York, urged that the flag be changed, to recognize the new states. Much debate ensued, since to add a star and a stripe every time a state was admitted would make the flag unwieldy. We are indebted to Congressman Wendover for his persistence. He called on a Captain Reid, then in the naval service of the United States, to design a flag that would be in keeping with the original intention of the Flag Act and that would at the same time permit recognition of new states. Captain Reid and Congressman Wendover corresponded for almost two years. Finally Captain Reid's suggestions were submitted to Congress in a bill and were accepted almost substantially as he advised. The bill was signed on April 4, 1818, by President Monroe. It read:

That from and after the fourth of July next the flag of the United States be thirteen horizontal stripes, alternate red and white; that the union be twenty stars white in a blue field.
. . . That on the admission of every new State into the Union one star be added to the union of the flag, and that such addition shall take effect on the fourth day of July next succeeding such admission.

One of Captain Reid's suggestions was that the twenty stars in the union be arranged to form one great star. This he thought would be in keeping with the phrase that the "stars represent a new constellation." Under his direction, the design he suggested was carried out by Mrs. Reid. This flag was presented to Congress and was the first one flown after the passage of the Flag Act. But arrangement of the stars in the union into one star did not meet with Congressional approval. With the addition of more stars, each star would have to be very small to fit into the design of one great star. Future flags appeared with the stars in rows, either directly under each other or arranged in checkerboard fashion, depending on whether there were an even or odd number of stars.

OLD GLORY

4

*Changes in the United States Flag
in 1818 and Thereafter*

By the law of 1818, the flag of the United States was fixed except for the disposition of the white stars in the blue canton. Changes in the number of stars in the canton were made as prescribed by law as the nation grew. Shortly after the act of 1818, Illinois became a state. She was admitted to the Union in December, 1818, and the following July her star was added to the flag. By 1820, two more stars had been added for Alabama and Maine. The twenty-fourth star was added in 1822 for Missouri.

The flag known as Old Glory may be seen in the Essex Institute at Salem. It is the flag containing twenty-four stars in the canton, and Captain William Driver of Salem, Massachusetts, in command of the brig *Charles Doggett,* is credited with naming it. As the brig was preparing to leave Salem, friends came aboard and presented Captain Driver with a large American flag. The flag was hoisted and when it unfurled, Captain Driver was moved to call it Old Glory. He continued to refer to the flag in that way, and the name Old Glory caught the people's fancy, probably because of its inspiring and affectionate quality.

Seven years elapsed without the addition of a new star. In 1836, the twenty-fifth was added for Arkansas. Michigan added the twenty-sixth in 1837, and Florida the twenty-seventh in 1845. Texas, the Lone Star state, entered the Union in 1846. Hers was the twenty-eighth star.

The annexation of Texas in 1846 was the occasion for the Mexican War. The flag of the United States at the beginning of the war contained twenty-eight stars, but while the war was still being fought Iowa asked to be admitted. The twenty-ninth star for Iowa appeared in the union in 1847, so that either the twenty-eight or the twenty-nine star flag can be called the United States flag during the Mexican War. On September 14, 1847, General Scott led his victorious army into Mexico City. Ten hours later the Stars and Stripes waved over the walls of the palace of Montezuma. On February 2, 1848, a treaty of peace conveyed to the United States all the territory in the west out of which were formed the states of California, Nevada, Utah, part of Colorado, and the greatest part of New Mexico and Arizona. The purchase from Mexico of the land that constitutes southern Arizona was arranged for by Captain Gadsden five years later.

The great amount of territory acquired during the Mexican War held forth the promise that many new states would be born. Meanwhile, Wisconsin was admitted in 1848, adding the thirtieth star to the flag. First of the new states from the West was California, whose admission in 1850 added the thirty-first star. In rapid succession, Minnesota in 1858, Oregon in 1859, and Kansas in 1861 entered the Union.

During the Civil War, no stars were removed from the flag. In fact, even while there was the possibility that the eleven stars of the Confederate states might vanish, new stars were constantly being added to the flag. West Virginia entered the Union in 1863 as the thirty-fifth state and Nevada in 1864 was the thirty-sixth.

Nebraska, admitted in 1867, saw its star, the thirty-seventh added that same year. A whole decade passed before the thirty-eighth star was added. It was for Colorado. An even longer period was to elapse before another addition to the flag, but there was ample recompense in 1889, when five states came into existence. North Dakota and South Dakota were admitted in that order, the thirty-ninth and fortieth states, then Montana, Washington, and Idaho. Idaho, the forty-third state, was admitted on July 3, 1890. By law a star was to be added on the fourth of July for all states admitted in the year ending on the third of July, so Idaho was entitled to have her star in the flag the very next day. Wyoming was admitted on July 10, 1890. Her star, the forty-fourth, was added in 1891. The forty-fifth star in our flag was added in 1896 for Utah.

Under date of March 18, 1896, a War Department Order was issued. It was signed by David S. Lamont, Secretary of War, and reveals an attempt to standardize the arrangement of the stars in the union. It reads:

The field or union of the National flag in use in the Army will, on and after July 4, 1896, consist of forty-five stars, in six rows, the first, third, and fifth rows to have eight stars, and the second, fourth, and sixth rows seven stars each, in a blue field, arranged as on the following page.

The following page shows them arranged in quincunx order, that is, like the black spaces on a checkerboard.

The War Department Order of 1896 is particularly worthy of notice because the Army had only recently begun to carry the Stars and Stripes as the national colors. For many years after the Army was reestablished in 1789, the national colors carried by the Army consisted of a blue field embroidered with an eagle. During the War of 1812, the flag carried by the various companies contained an eagle in whose breast was a striped shield. Recognition of the increased number of states comprising the United States of America appeared in the number of stars that surrounded the eagle's head. They numbered seventeen at this time. The Infantry was first given permission to carry the Stars and Stripes as national colors in 1841. Flags that had been used earlier then continued to be used by some as their regimental colors.

The same state of affairs existed in the United States Marine Corps. A flag carried by them during the Mexican War was embroidered with an eagle clasping a shield in its talons. Encircling the eagle and shield was a great circle consisting of twenty-four stars and, within, five stars in a parallel arc above the eagle's head. The Marines were first authorized to carry the Stars and Stripes as national colors in 1876. Eleven years later the Cavalry was given the right to carry our national flag.

The Army did not make its own flags, but contracted with private manufacturers to make them, so the flags lacked uniformity. The Navy, on the other hand, made its own flags from 1818 on, so that they were regulated and uniform. In 1896, when Secretary of War Lamont issued the order fixing the arrangement of the stars in the flag, Secretary Herbert of the Navy assented to the same arrangement.

During the Spanish American War, our fleets in the Atlantic and Pacific Oceans displayed the forty-five-star flag. It flew from the battleship *Maine,* blown up in Havana Harbor in 1898.

The admission of Oklahoma in November 1907 necessitated rearrangement of the stars. There were to be six rows in all. The first, third, fourth, and sixth rows were to have eight stars, the second and fifth rows seven stars each.

Two states, New Mexico and Arizona, were admitted in 1912. This brought the number of stars in the flag to forty-eight. As prescribed by the War and Navy Departments and with the approval of the President, the order was six rows of eight stars, each directly under the other. This arrangement must be considered final, both in the number of stars and their placement, unless our government changes the principle hitherto adhered to, that all the states of the Union must consist of contiguous continental territory, not of detached or outlying lands.

From the creation of the Navy under General Washington,

UNION JACK

the custom of flying small boat flags with only thirteen stars had persisted. By Presidential Order of 1916, this practice was discontinued. All flags, Army, Navy, and Government contain the full complement of forty-eight stars, eliminating another variation in our flag designs that persisted for so many years.

One other important flag that you will quickly identify as the canton of our Stars and Stripes is the Union Jack, a blue field bearing forty-eight white stars. It is flown from the bow of all ships of war while at anchor, from boats of the Navy carrying diplomatic officers whose rank is that of Charge d'Affaires or higher, and from boats afloat under the jurisdiction of the naval governors of Guam, Tutuila, and the Virgin Islands.

The significance of the colors in the flag of the United States was defined by the Continental Congress thus: "White signifies Purity and Innocence; Red Hardiness and Valor; Blue Vigilance, Perseverance and Justice." Ascribed to George Washington is this description of our flag,—"We take the stars from heaven, the red from our Mother Country, separating it by white stripes, thus showing that we have separated from her, and the white stripes shall go down to posterity representing Liberty."

The stars represent the states in the Union and have increased as the Union has grown but the thirteen stripes are a perpetual tribute to the original thirteen states who united and through their untiring efforts and zeal, created our nation, the United States of America.

A STAR FOR EVERY STATE

ORDER	STATE	DATE OF ADMISSION TO THE UNION	DATE STAR WAS ADDED TO THE FLAG
1.	Delaware	December 7, 1787	Stars for the
2.	Pennsylvania	December 12, 1787	first thirteen
3.	New Jersey	December 18, 1787	states were
4.	Georgia	January 2, 1788	originally
5.	Connecticut	January 9, 1788	placed in
6.	Massachusetts	February 6, 1788	the flag as
7.	Maryland	April 28, 1788	prescribed by
8.	South Carolina	May 23, 1788	the first Flag
9.	New Hampshire	June 21, 1788	Act of June 14,
10.	Virginia	June 26, 1788	1777,
11.	New York	July 26, 1788	which the
12.	North Carolina	November 21, 1789	Continental
13.	Rhode Island	May 29, 1790	Congress passed.
14.	Vermont	March 4, 1791	May 1, 1795
15.	Kentucky	June 1, 1792	May 1, 1795
16.	Tennessee	June 1, 1796	July 4, 1818
17.	Ohio	March 1, 1803	July 4, 1818
18.	Louisiana	April 30, 1812	July 4, 1818
19.	Indiana	December 11, 1816	July 4, 1818
20.	Mississippi	December 10, 1817	July 4, 1818
21.	Illinois	December 3, 1818	July 4, 1819
22.	Alabama	December 14, 1819	July 4, 1820
23.	Maine	March 15, 1820	July 4, 1820
24.	Missouri	August 10, 1821	July 4, 1822
25.	Arkansas	June 15, 1836	July 4, 1836
26.	Michigan	January 26, 1837	July 4, 1837
27.	Florida	March 3, 1845	July 4, 1845
28.	Texas	December 29, 1845	July 4, 1846
29.	Iowa	December 28, 1846	July 4, 1847
30.	Wisconsin	May 29, 1848	July 4, 1848
31.	California	September 9, 1850	July 4, 1851
32.	Minnesota	May 11, 1858	July 4, 1858
33.	Oregon	February 14, 1859	July 4, 1859
34.	Kansas	January 29, 1861	July 4, 1861
35.	West Virginia	June 19, 1863	July 4, 1863
36.	Nevada	October 31, 1864	July 4, 1865

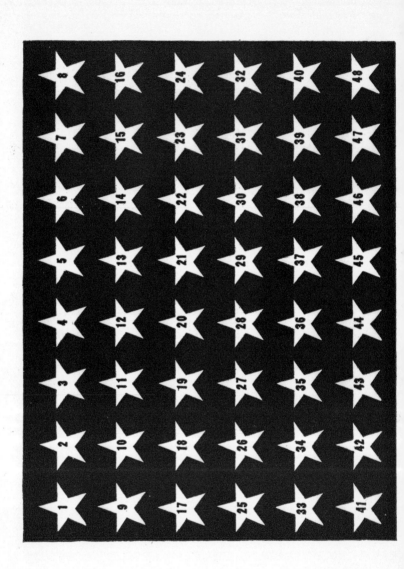

37.	Nebraska	March 1, 1867	July 4, 1867
38.	Colorado	August 1, 1876	July 4, 1877
39.	North Dakota	November 2, 1889	July 4, 1890
40.	South Dakota	November 2, 1889	July 4, 1890
41.	Montana	November 8, 1889	July 4, 1890
42.	Washington	November 11, 1889	July 4, 1890
43.	Idaho	July 3, 1890	July 4, 1890
44.	Wyoming	July 10, 1890	July 4, 1891
45.	Utah	January 4, 1896	July 4, 1896
46.	Oklahoma	November 16, 1907	July 4, 1908
47.	New Mexico	January 6, 1912	July 4, 1912
48.	Arizona	February 14, 1912	July 4, 1912

5

Flags of United States Territories and Dependencies

IN THE FIRST four chapters of this book, the growth of our country from a colonial dependency comprising thirteen English colonies to the United Colonies of America, out of which was created the United States of America has been traced to show how our national flag, the Stars and Stripes, evolved. The decades that followed bear testimony to the pioneering and industrious character of our ancestors and their families who migrated westward and to the attractiveness the "land of the free, and the home of the brave" had for the oppressed and the persecuted of other continents as well as for those whose opportunity was limited and defined.

In the year 1867, the United States acquired, for the first time, territory that was not contiguous to continental United States. This chapter is devoted to the flags of our two Territories, Alaska and Hawaii, and to the United States possessions that are designated dependencies, namely, Puerto Rico, Guam, Panama Canal Zone, and the Virgin Islands; their flag is the flag of the United States but they have individual flags that are always flown second to the Stars and Stripes.

ALASKA

ALASKA is a land of abundant resources, rich in minerals, forests, and streams. It was acquired by the United States in

1867 by purchase from Russia, and by an act of Congress of August 24, 1912, it was made a Territory.

The blue in the flag of Alaska signifies the evening sky, the blue of the sea and lakes, and the blue of wild Alaskan flowers; the gold, the wealth that lies hidden in Alaska's hills and streams.

The stars are arranged so that seven of them form the constellation Ursa Major, the Great Bear, which is the most conspicuous constellation in the Northern sky. Contained in the constellation are the Dipper and two Pointers, the two stars that form the outer side of the cup and that always point to Polaris, no matter in what position the Dipper may be. The eighth star in the flag is Polaris, the North Star, that ever-constant star for the mariner, explorer, hunter, trapper, prospector, woodsman, and surveyor.

HAWAII

In 1791, King Kamehameha established his throne and brought under his rule all the Hawaiian Islands, which were discovered by Captain James Cook in 1778. The English explorer George Vancouver presented King Kamehameha with an English flag, in 1793, and told him he could use it. Apparently he did for, in 1808, a traveler reported that he saw the British flag flying over the Hawaiian king's residence.

A new national banner was established by the Hawaiian Legislative Council on May 25, 1845, and this same banner

was later adopted in 1925 by the Territory of Hawaii. Its canton is a reproduction of the British Union Jack. Hawaii, Maui, Kahoolawe, Lanai, Molokai, Oahu, Nihau, and Kauai, the eight main islands comprising the Hawaiian group, are represented by the eight stripes of red, white, and blue.

A century after King Kamehameha ascended the throne the monarchy was overthrown and a republic declared. Then, by a joint resolution of Congress of July 7, 1898, the Hawaiian Islands were formally annexed to the United States. On June 14, 1900, Hawaii was made a Territory, and the Stars and Stripes became its national flag.

The old Hawaiian flag is used as a Territorial flag and is always flown second to the flag of the United States.

GUAM

GUAM, the largest of the Pacific island group known as the Marianas, was ceded to the United States by Spain in accordance with the Treaty of Paris of December 10, 1898. It is a dependency of the United States. Agaña is its capital.

The island is governed as a naval station. The Governor of Guam must be a naval officer. He is appointed by the President of the United States.

The flag of the Governor of Guam consists of a blue field with an elliptical figure edged in red in the center. Within the figure is shown a cocoanut tree against the horizon. Across the center of the ellipsis appears the name Guam in red letters. A sail boat approaches the shores where grows the cocoanut tree.

PANAMA CANAL ZONE

By the treaty of 1904, the United States acquired the Panama Canal Zone from the Republic of Panama, in consideration of certain payments and conditions.

The flag of the Governor of the Panama Canal Zone, established by Executive Order of President Wilson dated June 8, 1915, has the seal of the Canal Zone in the center of its blue field. The device on the shield is a ship under full sail about to pass through Gaillard Cut below Gold Hill and Contractor's Hill, and the motto on the streamer below the shield is, appropriately, "The land divided, the world united."

VIRGIN ISLANDS

The Virgin Islands, in the West Indies, were purchased by the United States from Denmark in 1917. There are three principal islands, St. Thomas, St. Croix, and St. John and several smaller ones. By an act of Congress of 1927, the natives of this U. S. dependency were given citizenship.

An order dated May 17, 1921, established the flag of the Virgin Islands. The American eagle grasps in his left talon a bundle of three blue arrows; in his right talon, a sprig of green laurel. And on his breast is the shield of the United States.

PUERTO RICO

PUERTO RICO, meaning Rich Coast, was discovered by Columbus in 1493. Ponce de Leon conquered the island in 1509 and became the first governor. In 1898, at the close of the Spanish American War, Spain ceded Puerto Rico to the United States by the treaty of Paris.

Puerto Rico does not have a flag of its own. When it was a Spanish possession, it flew the Spanish flag. The flag used by the Puerto Rican insurgents in 1898 and then adopted by Puerto Rico was almost a replica of the Cuban flag except that the colors were interchanged. The stripes were red and white, the triangle blue, and the star on it white.

An historic coat of arms appears, however, on the official seal and on the banner of the Governor General of the island. The device between the letters F and I, the yokes and arrows, is explained as a token of mutual affection between Ferdinand and Isabella, who chose these symbols because their initials were also those of the monarchs. The yoke, in Spanish yugo, is for Ysabella and the sheaf of arrows, in Spanish flechas, is for Ferdinand. "Joannes est nonem ejus," the motto that surrounds the lower half of the shield, means "His Name is John." Two lions and two castles on the border represent the kingdoms of Leon and Castile. The two flags bear devices from the coats of arms of the various kingdoms under the rule of Ferdinand and Isabella.

6

Flag Terminology

THE WORD FLAG is derived from the Anglo-Saxon word
fleogan, Dutch vlag, Swedish flagg, German flagge and Middle
English flakken. It is a generic term in the English language
and covers all forms—banners, ensigns, pendants, streamers
and others; when prefixed by the word national, it denotes
that piece of cloth, generally though not always rectangular
in shape, attached at one end to a pole, on which is displayed
the nation's distinctive device or color.

Flags such as we see today came into existence in the early
Middle Ages. The earliest flag resembled a totem pole and
was used by primeval man to represent his family. Man's
gregarious nature and his instinct for self-preservation caused
him and his family to band together with other families into
a tribe. The tribal chieftain organized the young men into
an army to defend the tribe when necessary. The standard
borne by the army was the standard of the chief of the tribe.
Gradually, tribes came together and united to form a state,
pooling the men from each for the protection of the whole.
The strength of each tribe lay in the army and its chief, the
ruler of the state.

As the state grew and its functions became more complex,
the power was transferred from hereditary successors to citizens who were best qualified to head the state and the army.
The army was subordinated to the state: it became the serv-
ant of the state and its citizenry. The imperial aspirations of

the Roman state extended the idea of nationality, bringing together under one standard peoples in other parts of the world. But the standards of the ancient world differed not only in their concepts of nationality but in their physical appearance.

The standards of the nations of antiquity were usually devices of wood or metal that were carried at the head of a spear or pole. The Bible contains many references wherein the members of the tribes of Israel are told to pitch camp close to their standards. The Egyptians carried staffs ornamented with such devices as animals that were considered sacred; streamers were attached to the staff below the device. The bull was sacred to the Assyrians, so their standards were ornamented with a circular disc on which the animal was painted. An eagle attached to a lance was used by the Persians, while the Greeks used emblems that were sacred because of their association with one of their deities or because they were legendary. Athenians bore a standard with an olive and an owl, Corinthians used pegasus as their emblem, the Messenians used the letter M, Thebans a sphinx, Boeotians a bull, and the Peloponnesians a tortoise.

Standards of the Roman legions were ornamented with minotaurs, wolves, horses, and bears. When Marius became consul, in the later days of the empire, he ordered that the Roman legions should carry the eagle as their standard to replace all others. With the fall of the Roman Empire, the decline of the ancient world, and the ascendancy of Christianity over pagan religions, the emblems that prevailed were religious in character, and were ornamented with various forms of the cross. These religious emblems have been perpetuated to this day in certain national flags as, for instance, the flag of Great Britain, which bears the crosses of St. George, St. Andrew, and St. Patrick.

The idea that each nationality must have its own flag, that this flag represent all the citizens of that nation and be in no way a personal banner of the king or chief of state, is a modern development. Most nations today have a flag that

35

symbolizes all the virtues that we know as patriotism. The national flag is the symbol of what a nation has done, what it aspires to do, and what, in practice, it idealizes. Let us look at our national flag with pride and with determination, drawing from it inspiration so to steer the ship of state that our descendants may continue to look at it with honor, with pride, and with respect.

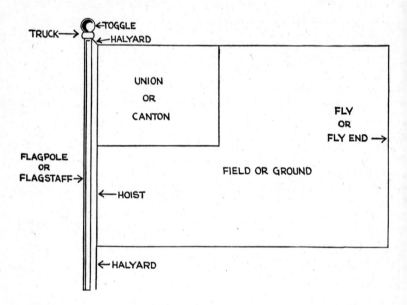

Flags are made up of several parts and each has its own name.

FLAGSTAFF OR FLAG POLE

The flagstaff or flag pole is the pole on which the flag is displayed.

TRUCK

The truck is the ornament, in the shape of a crown, a knob, or a cap, at the top of the flagstaff. It is generally a circular piece of wood at the extreme end of the flagstaff furnished with pulleys through which the halyards are reeved.

HALYARDS

Halyards are the ropes used to hoist and lower the flag and to secure it. They are given special names depending on their use. The halyards used to hoist a flag or ensign are, for instance, called ensign halyards.

HOIST

The hoist of a flag is that part along the flagstaff from which the flag is hoisted. It is, therefore, the height of the flag measured along the flag staff or halyard. In heraldic language, this part would be known as the head or chief. Hoist sometimes refers to that portion of the flag closer to the flagstaff, to distinguish it from the fly.

FLY

The fly is the breadth of the flag measuring it from the flagstaff to the outer edge. The word is also used to mean that portion of the flag farther from the flagstaff.

CANTON

The canton is the rectangular compartment occupying the upper left hand corner of the flag, next to the staff, wherein is placed the union, or national device. It may be as large as one quarter of the whole flag. Sometimes, the words canton and union are used interchangeably to mean this device, though canton is a French word meaning corner or angle and originally meant the space only.

UNION

The union is the device appearing in the canton. It is so called because it contains the symbol of unity. Thus the flag of the United States has a union representing the confederation of forty-eight states. The crosses of St. George, St. Andrew, and St. Patrick in the union of the British flag represent the union of the kingdoms of England, Scotland and Ireland. Flag descriptions often distinguish between the union of a flag and the fly, which in this case is the remainder of the flag.

According to the rules of heraldry, the blue field, that is the Union, is the honor point of the flag. Because of this, it is supposed to hold the position of danger. But the sword arm or right arm is the position of danger, which means that the Union of the flag, as it appears to the observer, should be to the flag's right.

An easy way to determine the correct way to display the flag is to remember that it is always spoken of as the Stars and Stripes. Therefore, one should always see the Stars before the Stripes.

GROUND

The ground is the background or base color of a shield or flag. It is synonymous with field.

FIELD

The field is the ground of the flag or the sections of it. In the description of the union in the flag of the United States, we say that it has a blue field with forty-eight white stars. The word is supposed to have originated from the circumstance that the surface of a shield was ornamented with symbols that a knight won through his deeds on the field of battle.

UNION JACK

The union jack is the union used separately as a flag. For example, the union jack used by the United States Navy is a blue field with forty-eight white stars; the union jack of Great Britain is a blue field having the crosses of St. George, St. Andrew, and St. Patrick on the whole. It is flown from the jackstaff in the bow of a vessel, which accounts for its being called a jack.

COLORS

The plural of the word color is used to denote the national flag. Regiments in the United States Army carry a pair of colors, the national colors and the regimental color. In parades, the regimental color is borne to the left of the national colors. Salute to the colors is the ceremony, accompanied by music, of saluting the national flag as it is hoisted in the morning and lowered in the evening.

KING'S COLORS

King's colors is another name for the British Union Jack.

ENSIGN

The ensign is the naval flag. Our rank of ensign in the United States Navy derives from the fact that men in that rank formerly were charged with the responsibility of bearing and caring for the flag. In the United States, the Stars and Stripes is the national, the military, and the naval flag, but in many countries the national flag is different from the ensign or the merchant flag.

FLAG PROPORTIONS

Flag proportions vary. There is no universal rule. Some flags are almost square, many are rectangular, either in the proportion of 3:2 or 2:1, and some of the Scandinavian countries have ensigns that are swallow-tailed or swallow-tailed with a tongue.

SWALLOW-TAILED

A swallow-tailed flag is a forked flag. It has a triangular piece cut out of the flag so that two tails are left at the fly end.

SWALLOW-TAILED WITH A TONGUE

A swallow-tailed flag with a tongue, or a triple swallow-tailed flag, is one that has three tails at the fly end, one top and bottom and one in the middle of the flag.

FLAG DESIGNS

Flag designs, according to the rules of heraldry, must be arranged so that color is not placed on color, or metal on metal. In blazonry, yellow is the equivalent of gold and white of silver. Blue and red, therefore, being colors, should always be separated by a metal, yellow or white. These rules are not always adhered to, as in the case of Venezuela, where the flag contains yellow, blue, and red stripes, the blue and red touching.

FLAG EXPRESSIONS

A few of the more common flag expressions are given below:

To "run up" a flag is to hoist a flag.

To "strike the flag" is to lower the flag at sea, or to take it down as a sign of surrender.

To "dip the flag" is to salute another nation or its representatives by lowering the flag and immediately hoisting it again. It is a symbol of respect, friendly courtesy, or welcome. Ships at sea usually salute each other by dipping their colors.

To "break a flag." On special occasions a flag is broken. The flag is first folded then rolled and hoisted, and so secured that it will be broken by a pull on the halyard at a given signal.

To "hoist the flag reversed" is to hoist the flag with the union down. It is done to signal distress.

A great many flags contain badges, arms, and embellishments. Certain technical terms have been employed in describing flags so adorned, although an attempt has been made to use these as sparingly as possible.

SURMOUNTED

Surmounted is the adjective used to describe a charge that has a device of another color or metal on it.

BEARING

Bearing is an animal, object, or figure with which the shield is charged. A shield can contain one or more bearings depending on whether it is quartered or otherwise divided.

CHARGE

To charge means to put a bearing or device on a shield or flag. The Italian flag is an example. It is charged with the arms of the house of Savoy.

DISPLAYED

Displayed is the adjective used to describe a bird of prey with its wing spread, erect, and with its breast exposed to the observer. It is frequently used to describe an eagle thus portrayed and is synonymous with the term "spread eagle."

BADGE

The badge is a distinguishing emblem, such as appears in the fly of the flag of Newfoundland. It is borne alone, without any shield or other accessory, although it may be accompanied by a motto.

ARMS

The arms, known also as ensigns armorial, properly consist of shield, supporters, crest, and motto. The *shield* is ornamented with figures and colors that are marks of family distinction and achievement. *Supporters* are human beings, animals, or objects placed at either side of the shield to support it. Two reasons for their existence are given: one is that a knight, when he entered a joust, left his shield to be held up by two retainers, who often dressed themselves as animals. The other is that seal engravers, in their desire to leave no vacant spaces between the sides of the shield and the arc of the circle, filled them in with a pair of animals or other figures. The *crests* were plumes or tufts on the heads of birds originally. They were placed for ornamentation on the top of the helm, thus forming the crest. Other devices that could be used to ornament the helm began to be used. Often a crown was used because it was adaptable; it became associated with one family or country, but purely as ornaments, having no connection with the rank or peerage of its owner. The *mottoes* are the "words" or "reasons" on the arms, either on the scroll or on the shield itself. *Quartering* of the shield is done to combine the arms of two or more persons or families. According to the rules of heraldry, the first and fourth quarters should be alike, and the second and third.

ESCUTCHEON

An escutcheon is a smaller shield with which the main shield is charged. Escutcheon may also refer to the complete coat of arms. An *escutcheon of pretense* is a small shield displaying the coat of arms of an heiress. The Rumanian coat of arms has an escutcheon of pretense. Here the arms of the heiress are not impaled with her husband's, that is, placed side by side with his on the shield, but appear in a small shield in the center.

DEXTER AND SINISTER

The dexter side of the shield is the right side. The sinister side, the left side of the shield. Therefore, the dexter side of a shield, to an observer, would appear on his left, the sinister on his right.

Passant, respectant, statant, rampant, regardant are used to describe the attitudes of beasts of prey, of which the lion is the most frequently used. Inasmuch as so many of the coats of arms contained in the flags of European nations contain the figure of a lion, these terms are explained.

PASSANT

A lion passant is a lion walking, with his right paw upraised.

RESPECTANT

Lion respectant designates two animals who are facing each other as if in combat.

Lion statant is a lion standing with all four feet on the ground.

A lion rampant is a lion standing upright on one foot. Usually the lion is shown with his head to the right of the shield. If his head is in another position, then he is described as gardant, regardant.

A lion rampant gardant is shown full face.

A lion rampant regardant has his head turned toward his tail.

A demilion is the upper half of a lion in upright position, used as a charge.

The saltire is a diagonal cross, or a cross in the form of an X, such as the cross of St. Andrew.

Oriflamme may mean a glorious or royal symbol. One of the best known is the oriflamme of France. It was a scarlet flag with three tails, to which were attached tassels of green silk. This banner hung in the abbey of St. Denis over the tomb of St. Denis. It is probable that it replaced the Chape de Martin as the national flag of France sometime after the kings of France had the seat of government transferred to Paris, where St. Denis was held in high esteem. Louis VI is said to have borne the oriflamme into battle in 1124. Its last appearance on the field of battle was in 1415 at Agincourt.

7

Flags of Foreign Nations

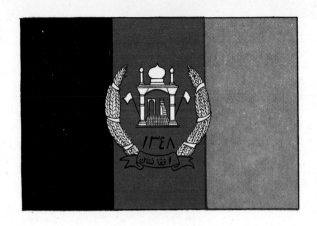

AFGHANISTAN

AFGHANISTAN, in southern Asia, won its independence on August 19, 1919, but it was not until King Nadir Khan came into power in October, 1929, that the national flag was adopted.

The black in the flag was chosen to signify progress from darkness, the red indicates sacrifice, and the green, prosperity. Nearly all Afghans are Mohammedans. The oriental open mosque revealing a pulpit and a mihrab are symbolic of their religion, as the church and altar are of the Christian world.

The sprays of wheat that issue from either side of the mosque signify the dominant industry of the country, agriculture.

Afghanistan is written in Persian on the scroll. The writing below the mosque and the scroll is in Persian, too. It is the date 1348 of the Hejira year, reckoned according to the Mohammedan calendar, and is the equivalent of 1929 A.D. in the Christian calendar. It is the year King Nadir Khan ascended the throne.

ALBANIA

THE NATIONAL FLAG of Albania was adopted in 1913 following the Treaty of November 28, 1912, by which Albania gained her independence. Perhaps it would be more accurate to say that the flag was readopted in 1913. It existed much earlier but as long as Albania was a subject country, it flew the flag of the ruling country.

The Albanians, the oldest race in southeastern Europe, were conquered by the Turks in 1431 and but for a brief period were dominated by them until 1913.

George Castriotes, an ancient Albanian beloved by his countrymen and regarded by them as their national hero, was educated in Turkey but yearned to make his country free. He led his countrymen against the forces of the Sultan, and on the Illyrian hillsides they fought and defeated the Turks. The Sultan acknowledged Castriotes as ruler of Albania in 1463 but before the year was out Albania was again under Turkish domination.

Castriotes, or Skanderbeg as he is more frequently called, designed the flag of Albania. Legend has it that the Albanians are the descendants of a mountain eagle. Moreover,

46

the Albanian name for Albanians is Shgipetar which means "descendants of a mountain eagle." Thus Skanderbeg decided that the doubleheaded eagle should be the national emblem.

Other nations in that part of the world have used the black doubleheaded eagle. The reason advanced is that it represented sovereignty over the East and the West. The nations using it were then situated in the middle of the known Eastern and Western world.

ANDORRA

ANDORRA is a small principality situated in the Pyrenees between France and Spain. Although the country ruled itself for over six hundred years, it did not have a national flag until the middle of the nineteenth century.

Many hundreds of years ago Andorra was given its independence by Charlemagne in return for its help to him in his campaign against the Moors. Then in 1278, Andorra was placed under the joint suzerainty of the French Count of Foix and the Spanish Bishop of Urgel. By marriage, the French rights passed to the House of Beárn and with the accession of Henry IV they passed to the French crown. When France changed from a monarchy to a republic, the rights were vested in the President of the French Republic.

In 1806, Napoleon granted Andorra a constitution and it became a republic. Andorra gave itself a national flag, but it still considers itself under the joint sovereignty of the President of France (acting for the House of Foix) and the Spanish Bishop of Urgel. Two judges appointed by the Spanish Bishop of Urgel and the President of France have judicial power in civil affairs. A council composed of Andorrans is elected to govern the country.

The first flag of Andorra was divided vertically, the half near the hoist gold, the half in the fly red. These were the colors of the House of Foix, protectors of the state, and were chosen in their honor. Subsequently the flag was changed. The red and gold representing the House of Foix were retained and the stripes were arranged horizontally. A coronet, which is the crown of a count, was imposed on the yellow stripe, since nominally a count was its ruler.

ARGENTINA

THE NATIONAL FLAG of Argentina was adopted in 1816. The origin of the blue and white in it can be found in events of 1807, when the British attempted to invade Buenos Aires. They were repulsed by regiments of Argentine militia who called themselves the Patricios. The Patricios wore uniforms of blue and white.

Discontent with Spanish rule was responsible for the formation of a secret society of Argentine intellectuals and leaders who agitated for the establishment of local government. When, in 1810, the viceroy in the name of King Ferdinand VII issued a decree closing the port of Buenos Aires to commerce, the members of the society felt that the moment for revolt had arrived.

On the bleak and cloudy morning of May 25, 1810, the people gathered in the Plaza de Mayo and insisted on the right to a government of their choice. Two men active in the movement for freedom were in that crowd. They recalled the colors used by the Patricios and hastily made their way to a shop on the Plaza. There they purchased all the blue and white ribbon available and cut it into strips. They tucked pieces of the colors in their hatbands and rushed back to distribute the rest to the assembled patriots.

As the day wore on, these same two men petitioned the viceroy and his cabildo that a local governing body composed of men whose names they had on a list be appointed. In answer the viceroy called forth the militia to disband the multitude. The militia refused. It was then that the members of the cabildo went out onto the balcony and read the petition, calling for an expression of the will of the people. It is reported that just as the people shouted their approval, the sun broke through the clouds and shone down on them. This is the radiant sun, otherwise known as the Sol de Mayo or sun of May, that appears on the flag.

In 1812, General Manuel Belgrano ordered his regiments to wear blue and white cockades and carry a blue and white flag. The flag was adopted as the national flag of Argentina in 1816 by the Congress of Tucumán while that body met to draw up the Declaration of Independence.

AUSTRALIA

AUSTRALIA was explored by Captain James Cook in 1770. Eight years later the first English colonists settled on its coast and soon were pushing into the interior. By 1850, there were several colonies, each quite large and active in commerce. The need for some federal government to regulate these matters was recognized, but as the colonies could not agree upon the form, the union of the colonies was delayed. In 1899, a constitution was submitted and ratified by all and the federation of the colonies into the Commonwealth of Australia was effected in 1901.

The Commonwealth of Australia is the federation of the seven states of New South Wales, Victoria, Queensland, South Australia, Western Australia, Tasmania and the Northern Territory. It is a part of the British Empire and has the status of a dominion.

The national flag of Australia is officially the British Union Jack. The blue ensign of Australia is commonly used by Australians on national holidays and celebrations. Its five seven-pointed stars in the field form the constellation of the Southern Cross. The large seven-pointed star under the union was originally six-pointed in 1903, when the flag came into use. With the creation of the seventh state designated the Northern Territory, the star was changed to a seven-pointed star, each point representing a state in the Commonwealth of Australia.

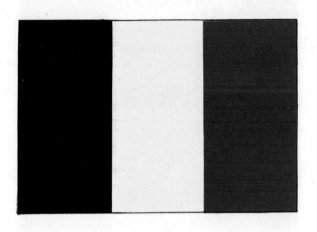

BELGIUM

THE NATIONAL FLAG of Belgium, in its present form, was adopted on January 23, 1831. That is the year Belgium formulated its constitution and became a constitutional hereditary monarchy.

The three colors of the flag can be traced to the coat of arms of the duchy of Brabant, which had a yellow lion, with red tongue and claws, on a black field.

The history of Belgium before it became independent was closely linked with the Netherlands, Austria, and France. The duchy of Brabant, now the part of Belgium in which the capital city of Brussels is situated, played a large part in the creation of the Belgian monarchy. From this province in 1830, a movement of revolt against the Netherlands started. Therefore, when Belgium became independent, it adopted for the flag the colors of the coat of arms of the ancient duchy of Brabant. The coat of arms of the duchy of Brabant became the armorial bearings of the King of Belgium.

BOLIVIA

ORIGINALLY, as Upper Peru, the territory that is now the Republic of Bolivia was liberated by General Simon Bolívar. With his patriot army, he fought the battles of Junin and Ayacucho successfully and put an end to Spanish domination in South America. In honor of General Bolívar's part in liberating it, the Congress of Upper Peru voted to name the country the Republic of Bolívar, but in conformity with his wishes it was named Bolivia. Bolívar has frequently been referred to as the "Washington of South America" because of his work in liberating Bolivia, Colombia, Ecuador, and Peru, and his untiring efforts to federate the South American republics. General Antonio José de Sucre, a Venezuelan by birth and a disciple of Bolívar, was equally active with Bolívar in the establishment of Bolivia and was chosen its first president.

The colors of the national flag of Bolivia were adopted in 1825 at Sucre, a city named in honor of General José de Sucre. Red in the flag denotes the animal kingdom, yellow the mineral kingdom, and green the vegetable kingdom. Mining is Bolivia's principal industry and during the two hundred years (from the middle of the sixteenth to the middle of the eighteenth centuries) when the country was under Spanish rule, great quantities of gold were extracted for the mother country.

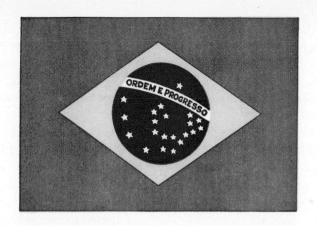

BRAZIL

THE FLAG of Brazil is symbolic of the rich natural heritage of the Brazilian nation and of its beginnings. The blue and white in the flag bring to mind Portugal, the mother country of Brazil, and the early Portuguese explorer, Pedro Alvarez Cabral, who around 1500 embarked on a voyage to find the Portuguese Indies and instead reached Brazil.

In 1899 the present Republic of Brazil was established. Before then, it had been ruled by an emperor, Pedro I, who was the son of the ruler of Portugal. The flag used in imperial days was green and had a yellow diamond in the center, as it does now, but differed in that it had a shield with sprigs of tobacco and coffee on either side and a royal crown above it.

Green and yellow, the national colors of Brazil, represent two of Brazil's natural resources: the green the vegetable kingdom, the yellow the mineral. The blue sphere dotted with stars, which form the constellation of the Southern Cross, represent the heavens as they may be observed at the capital of Brazil when the Southern Cross is at the meridian.

In addition to the five stars that form the Southern Cross,

there are sixteen others. The twenty-one stars stand for the twenty states composing the United States of Brazil and for its capital city, Rio de Janeiro. They stand, also, for civic independence and cooperation. The white band encircling the sphere marks the course of the terrestrial orbit. "Ordem e Progresso," the inscription on the band, means "Order and progress."

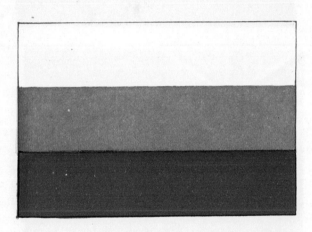

BULGARIA

THE BULGARIANS are an old Balkan people with a long record of national achievement, a record that has often been lost sight of during the subjection of the Bulgarians by the Turks through five whole centuries.

Bulgaria's first step toward independence was made in 1878, when, after the Russo-Turkish war, it became a self-ruling principality subject to the suzerainty of the Sultan of Turkey. Complete independence was attained by Bulgaria on October 5, 1908. The country then was ruled by a king and a national assembly consisting of one hundred sixty members who were elected to it by the people.

The national flag of Bulgaria was adopted by the Bulgarian Constituent Assembly, in 1878, at Tirnova. The red is supposed to represent the blood shed in the fight for freedom and the bravery and heroism of the Bulgarian Army; the white peace, and the green the fertility of the Bulgarian land, for Bulgaria is an agricultural country.

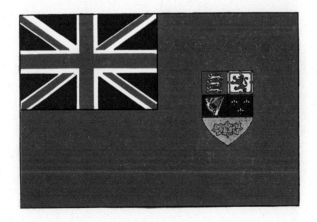

CANADA

The national flag of Canada, like the national flag of all the countries that form the British Commonwealth of Nations, is the British Union Jack, flag of the mother country.

Canada has a distinctive merchant flag, however, which is equally well known. This flag is the Red Ensign of Great Britain with the coat of arms of Canada in the fly. The first of the British dominions to create a merchant flag of its own,

Canada was granted the right to place her arms on the red ensign in 1892.

The arms were adopted in 1869, at which time the Dominion of Canada consisted of four provinces, Ontario, Quebec, New Brunswick, and Nova Scotia. The arms of Canada are a combination of the arms of the provinces. Canada's arms were superseded in 1921 by a complete achievement, that is, arms, crest, supporters, and motto.

The badge that appears in the flag today consists of a shield quartered; England is represented in the first quarter by three yellow lions, Scotland in the second quarter by a red lion rampant, Ireland in the third quarter by the Irish harp, and France in the fourth quarter by the fleur de lis. These symbols were chosen in recognition of the different national stocks from which the pioneers of Canada came. The maple leaves at the base of the shield are distinctively Canadian. The first French settlers arrived in Canada in the fall. They were so impressed with the beauty and color of the maple trees which grew throughout all of Canada, that they frequently used this design for embroidery and decoration.

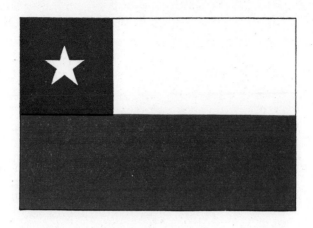

CHILE

THE FIRST ATTEMPT by Chilean patriots to gain independence and to throw off the yoke of Spain was made on September 18, 1810, at Santiago. The patriots deposed the Spanish captain-general and set up a provisional government. In 1812, General Carrera, the supreme director of Chile, adopted a rosette of blue, white, and yellow as the emblem of the nation then fighting for its freedom. A banner of these colors was raised in Santiago at the side of the flag of the United States on July 4, 1812, at a celebration in honor of its neighbor republic.

This flag was replaced by a flag of red, white, and blue on February 12, 1817, after Generals San Martín and O'Higgins defeated the Spaniards at Chacabuco. Later that year, on October 18th, General Bernardo O'Higgins decreed that the Chilean flag be red, white, and blue and the design of the present flag was established.

The origin of the red, white, and blue flag according to legend is that the armies of the Spanish conquerors used banners of these colors in their encounters with the Araucanian Indians who lived in the southern part of Chile.

Chilean historians, however, say that the choice of colors for the flag was influenced and inspired by the flag of the United States. The silver star against the blue field is the celestial symbol that was used in their banner by the Chilean Indians. It was incorporated in the flag to represent them.

CHINA

IMPERIAL CHINA, whose recorded history dates back five thousand years, had many flags. Generally they were yellow and were distinguished by a dragon. Modern times witnessed the development of a republican form of government in China, and with this change came changes in the flag.

The five colors in the first flag of the Chinese Republic stood for China and its provinces, namely: red for China, yellow for Manchuria, blue for Mongolia, white for Tibet, and black for Turkestan.

A strong nationalist movement was making itself felt in China. Its leader and spokesman was Chiang Kai-shek, head of the Kuomintang. His government established itself at Nanking in 1928, and one of the first acts of the new government was the adoption of a flag, the same one China uses at present.

Red, the background color of this flag, was retained because it had represented China proper in the earlier flag. The sun against a blue sky is symbolic of the prosperity which the new government hoped the nation would realize. Blue and white symbolize purity and justice respectively.

The twelve rays of the sun, the whole of which is the emblem of the Kuomintang, are also said to symbolize the twelve months of the year and the twelve periods of the Chinese day (it is divided into intervals of two hours). They signify that Chinese belief in freedom, happiness, and peace is as enduring as time and the shining sun.

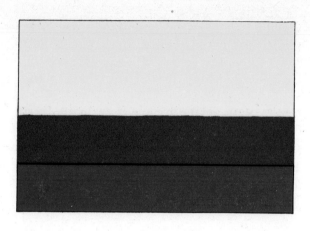

COLOMBIA

In common with four other South American republics, Colombia's independence was secured through the efforts of General Simon Bolívar. The national hero of Colombia is General Francisco de Paula Santander for it was he who joined the patriot army of Bolívar and led the army, in 1818, across the Andes. At Boyaca, a year later, their armies fought the battle that resulted in the liberation of Colombia, then known as New Granada.

The armies of Bolívar carried a banner of yellow in the upper half and blue and red stripes in the lower half. This flag was designed in 1806 by General Francisco de Miranda, famed for his devotion to the cause of South American independence. The flag was first flown from the *Leander,* a ship lying off the Haitian coast, on March 12, 1806. The ship was being outfitted for an expedition to liberate Spain's colonial possessions in South America. General Miranda's purpose was to create a flag that could be used by all of South America after independence had been achieved. It was his hope that every South American country would become a state and that the states would unite to form the nation.

The country liberated by Bolívar and Miranda was first called Greater Colombia. When Bolívar died in 1830, Greater Colombia ceased to exist. Three independent republics came into existence: Ecuador, Venezuela, and New Granada, which today is Colombia. The flags of all three still carry the colors of the Bolívarian flag.

Spain is the inspiration for the yellow and red in the flag. Yellow also represents the great mineral wealth of the country, red the blood shed by its heroes. The blue stripe symbolizes the waters of the Pacific Ocean and the Caribbean Sea, which touch the shores of Colombia.

COSTA RICA

Costa Rica was settled by the Spanish in 1540, and for almost three hundred years theirs was the only flag flown in Costa Rica. In 1821, Costa Rica secured her independence from Spain but was immediately annexed to Iturbide's Mexican Empire, of which she was a part until 1823, when the Empire was dissolved. On May 1, 1823, Costa Rica adopted her first flag. It was white with a red star in the center.

When the Central American Federation was formed, Costa Rica joined it. Thereafter, her flag was the Federation's blue, white, blue flag. When the Federation came to an end in 1838, the states composing it elected to be independent.

Costa Rica's next flag was adopted on April 21, 1840. It consisted of three horizonal stripes of white, blue, and white with the arms of Costa Rica in the center. The arms consisted of a radiant star against a celestial background.

On September 28, 1848, Costa Rica adopted a new flag, the flag it has used ever since. The five stripes are said to represent the five provinces into which the country is divided. Blue and white were retained in the flag because they appeared in the flag of the Federation. The broad red stripe denotes liberty.

CUBA

THE SPANIARDS had several names for the Pearl of the Antilles
—Juana, Santiago, and Ave Maria. But the name Cuba, by
which its early Indian inhabitants knew it, persisted even
through four hundred years of Spanish domination.

The Cubans fretted under Spanish rule and insurrections
were frequent. In 1848, General Narciso López, a Venezuelan soldier of fortune living in the United States, gathered
together some Cuban exiles and American sympathizers with
Cuba's cause and in 1849 and 1851 he led filibuster expedi-
tions to Cuba, purportedly to help Cuba gain its independence. Some historians say that the expedition, which
included men from Texas and other slave states, really
wanted Cuba annexed to the United States in the interest of
the slave holders. The expedition landed in Cuba and
hoisted the Lone Star flag, the flag of Cuba today. This flag
was adopted from the flag of the old Republic of Texas.

The Ten Years War that began in 1868 found the Cubans
using a flag of the same colors as the flag carried by López
but different in design. Half a year later, the López flag was
rediscovered and was officially adopted by the Cuban Con-

stituent Assembly. Cuba achieved her independence with the aid of the United States in 1898, at the close of the Spanish American War.

La Estrellita Solitaria, as the Cubans call the flag, was adopted by the Cuban Republic on May 20, 1902. The three blue stripes are said to represent, on the one hand, the three parts of the island, on the other, science, virtue, and beauty. The red stands for republicanism, and the white for purity. The triangle signifies equality and the star is the star of independence.

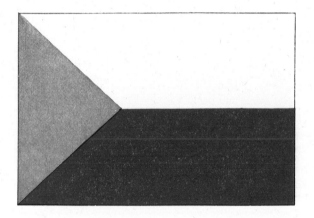

CZECHOSLOVAKIA

CZECHOSLOVAKIA was established as a republic at the end of World War I. Its independence was proclaimed on October 28, 1918. The constitution and flag of the new republic came into existence about 1920, and the flag was officially adopted March 30, 1930.

For an explanation of the colors in the national flag of

Czechoslovakia, it is necessary for us to know something about the history of the Czechs and the Slovaks. In the ninth century A.D. they composed a state known as the Great Moravian Empire. In the tenth century, the state was invaded by the Magyars. Next the Czechs formed the state of Bohemia. The Slovaks were in Hungary. In 1526, the King of Bohemia and Hungary was killed in battle, and the Bohemian crown fell to the Hapsburg monarchy. For the next five hundred years, Bohemia and Hungary were part of the Austro-Hungarian empire. Their struggle for freedom ended with the end of World War I.

The blue in the flag stands for Moravia. It was the color of that ancient state. The red and white were chosen for the flag because they were the ancient colors of the Kingdom of Bohemia. The blue peak, which has its base on the hoist and meets the red and white of Bohemia, is the emblem of the Carpathians.

DENMARK

THE EARLY HISTORY of Denmark begins about 800 A.D. Prior to that time we have sagas telling us about the deeds of early Scandinavian heroes.

The national flag of Denmark—it is called the Dannebrog —is said to be the oldest national ensign in the world. There are known to be earlier flags but they are no longer in use.

The legend concerning the Dannebrog is that it fell from heaven while King Waldemar II of Denmark and his men were fighting the Estonians during the battle of Lyndantse (now Reval) in 1219 in which the Estonians were defeated. Another legend says that King Waldemar II prayed for divine assistance while fighting the battle of Lyndantse. As he looked to the sky, he saw or believed he saw a white cross. Straightway he adopted the sign for the national flag and called it the Dannebrog, meaning the strength of Denmark.

It is believed that red was chosen as the color of the background because King Waldemar II thought that he saw the cross against a red sky although the illusion may have been caused by the blood he saw around him.

DOMINICAN REPUBLIC

THE NATIONAL FLAG of the Dominican Republic was designed by Juan Pablo Duarte, founder of the Dominican Republic, in 1838, when he organized the society called La Trinitaria whose efforts led to the independence of the country in 1844. The flag was hoisted in the Baluarte del Conde, Ciudad Trujillo, for the first time on February 27, 1844, the day the Dominicans revolted against their oppressors. The coat of arms of the Dominican Republic that appears in the flag was also conceived by Duarte. It was one of the items established by the Constitution adopted at San Cristobal in 1844, after independence from Spain had been achieved.

The significance of the colors in the flag (the colors repeat themselves in the shield) are: the red quarters mean Country, the blue ones mean God, and the white cross signifies Liberty.

The background of the coat of arms is a shield that tells of the struggle and resolution of the people to gain and preserve their independence. Above the shield, the streamer bearing the words "Dios, Patria, Libertad" means "God, country, liberty." This motto was the secret password of the members of La Trinitaria. The Holy Bible in the center of the shield is symbolic of light and truth. It is a call to unity for survival, inspired by the Gospel of Saint John. Four national flags, two on either side of the Bible, represent triumph. The gold cross surmounting the Bible tells of the redemption of the Dominican people from slavery. The spears are a symbol of the nobility of the soldier and the military proud. The two branches that surround the shield—one palm and the other laurel—are the emblems of glory and immortality.

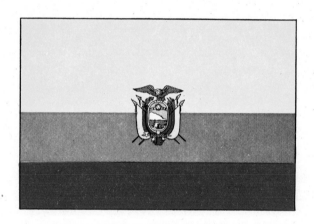

ECUADOR

ECUADOR LIES in the region of the equator as its name implies. In ancient times, it was ruled by the Caras who were succeeded by the Incas. Spanish rule prevailed with the decline of the Inca Empire. Ecuador's first attempt to gain independence, in 1809, was abortive. The revolution at Guayaquil in 1820 was the turning point. Generals Bolívar and

Sucre arrived upon the scene and the battle of Pichincha, in 1822, marked the beginning of Ecuador's independence.

In 1822, when Bolívar formed the Republic of Greater Colombia, a confederation of Ecuador, Colombia and Venezuela, Greater Colombia adopted for its flag the yellow, blue, and red flag designed by General Miranda and adopted by General Bolívar on June 5, 1811, for his patriot armies.

The three republics into which Greater Colombia was subsequently divided all retained Bolívar's colors in their flags. From 1830 to 1900, Ecuador adopted several flags. Then, in 1900, it was decreed that the flag of 1811 be the national flag of Ecuador.

Ecuador's interpretation of the colors is that yellow represents rich America (referring to the gold that was discovered), blue represents the ocean and red is for Spain. The significance of the order is that America is separated from Spain by the ocean.

The shield has depicted on it the sun and signs of the Zodiac for March, April, May, and June because events of great national importance occurred in these months. Mt. Chimborazo, the highest peak in Ecuador, is shown on the lower part of the shield. It played an important part in the war for independence. The steamship on the river is symbolic of trade and navigation. Above the shield is the condor, a bird native to the Andes. It is the equivalent of our American eagle—symbol of power. Branches of palm and laurel represent peace and glory. Under the shield, the bundle of consular fasces is emblematic of republican dignity.

EGYPT

EGYPT, the gift of the Nile as the Greeks called it, is a country sixty centuries old. In modern times, it was a part of the Turkish empire until 1914, when Great Britain made it a protectorate, dismissing the Khedive of Egypt and setting up instead a Sultan. In 1922, Egypt became independent and sovereign and in 1923 the national flag of Egypt, now in use, was adopted.

During the time that Egypt was part of the Turkish Empire, the Egyptian flag was similar to the Turkish flag. It was red, but with three white crescents, each enveloping a white star. When Egyptian independence was achieved, the flag was changed.

As Egypt was an agricultural country and green is symbolic of agriculture, the ground of the flag was made green. The crescent, a symbol of Mohammedanism, was incorporated in the flag because most Egyptians are Moslems. Mohammedan countries base their calendar on the lunar system: their months begin with the new moon and end with the full moon. The crescent, being one aspect of the moon by which Mohammedans reckon time, is used in most Mohammedan flags. So, too, the stars. There is apparently no significance to the number, three, of the stars in the Egyptian flag except inasmuch as this combination further distinguishes it from the Turkish flag.

EL SALVADOR

EL SALVADOR WAS DISCOVERED by Pedro de Alvarado, a Spaniard, in 1524. The country was inhabited by Indians and to this day a large part of the population is Indian. Many of the Maya Indians still live there.

El Salvador was a vice royalty of Guatemala and a Spanish possession until 1821, when, having secured its independence from Spain, it became a part of the Mexican Empire. El Salvador joined the Central American Federation when it was formed.

At the dissolution of the Federation in 1838, El Salvador continued to use the Federation flag for her own. In 1865, she finally replaced that flag with a flag composed of five

73

stripes of blue and white. The canton of this flag, red with fourteen stars, represented the fourteen territorial departments into which the Republic was divided.

In 1912, El Salvador decided to adopt the flag of the Federation again but with certain changes, one of which was the addition of her coat of arms. Thus the national flag of El Salvador conserves the flag of the Central American Federation.

The five volcanoes in the coat of arms represent the five states that composed the Federation. They represent, too, the mountainous nature of this country. The rainbow signifying hope and promise surmounts a cap of liberty, the symbol of freedom. Around the liberty cap is the inscription "15 de Septiembre de 1821," the date of the declaration of independence of several nations from Spanish rule and for that reason a date that appears in the arms of many Latin American countries. The inscription "Republica de El Salvador en la America Central," means "Republic of El Salvador in Central America." On a scroll beneath the triangle appears the motto of the Republic, "Dios Union Libertad," meaning "God, union, and liberty." The laurel branches surrounding the triangle are symbolic of glory.

ESTONIA

ESTONIA GAINED her independence by the Treaty of Tartu on February 2, 1920, after seven hundred years of subjection to various countries including Germany, Denmark, Sweden, Poland, and Russia. From 1710 to 1917, Estonia was ruled by the Czars of Russia.

About fifty years before Estonia became independent, there came into existence in that country strong cooperative movements. One of the first Estonian Students' Associations to be formed was organized as a cooperative. Beside the economic aspects of its activities, the Association fostered and, in a sense, crystallized the nationalist yearnings of the people. On September 17, 1881, the Estonian Students' Association adopted a flag.

The Russian government ordered the organization to dissolve. It took another name and continued, eventually becoming just a society. The flag of the Estonian Students' Association was so popular and was so closely associated with the desire for independence that Estonia adopted it as the national flag when the country became free. Before that time it had been used by all Estonians at any celebration or on any occasions that were national in character.

75

The significance of the three colors of the flag, originally chosen by Estonian students, has remained the same. The blue in the flag stands for the sky, the black for the rich soil, and the white for the snow that blankets the land of the Estonians throughout the long months of winter. It is said that the blue also represents mutual confidence, the black the dark period of suffering which the Estonians experienced, and the white hope.

ETHIOPIA

ETHIOPIA is both the ancient and the present name of the country that for a time was known as Abyssinia. It is one of the oldest states in the world. Its emperor is called the King of Kings, and the country is ruled by princes whom the king chooses. Its capitol is Addis Ababa. Some of its people are Christians, but the greater number are Mohammedans.

Ethiopia is primarily an agricultural country. Railroads have been built, but materials are still transported by caravans.

The national flag of Ethiopia came into use in the nineteenth century. Since ancient times Ethiopia has had a flag but, in a sense, it was not what we properly call a flag. It consisted of three separate pennants flown in the order in which the colors are arranged in the present flag. The pennants seem to have originated with the Ethiopian troops, each unit of which used a different pennant. It is reported that an Ethiopian mission that was sent to France in 1898 flew the colors as a flag for the first time.

One explanation of the colors in the flag is that the green symbolizes fertility of the land, yellow stands for the Abyssinians' love of country and their zeal for it, and the red signifies willingness to shed their blood in its defense. Another is that the colors represent the sections of Ethiopia: red for Tigre, yellow for Amhara, and green for Goa.

FINLAND

FROM 1154 to 1809, Finland was part of the Swedish kingdom. Then it was organized as an autonomous Grand Duchy of Russia. On December 6, 1917, Finland declared its independence from Russia. And on July 17, 1919, it became a republic. The national flag was approved by the Diet of Finland on May 29, 1918, although a flag of almost identical design was first approved in 1581.

The flag of Finland before 1581 did not have any coat of arms. In 1581, while Finland was under Sweden, King Johann III approved the flag containing the coat of arms at the intersection of the cross. The cross in the flag was chosen to symbolize Christianity. Red and yellow were the original national colors of Finland. The nine white roses represent the nine provinces that composed Finland. As a symbol of authority, the golden lion, wearing a Grand Duchy crown, was placed in the seal. The lion treads on a Russian scimitar. When Finland became independent, the crown of a Grand Duchy was removed from the lion to indicate that Finland now is a republic.

The blue in the flag stands for the blue of the lakes of Finland. So numerous are these, that Finland often has been called the Land of the Thousand Lakes. The white is symbolic of the snow-covered fields of Finland.

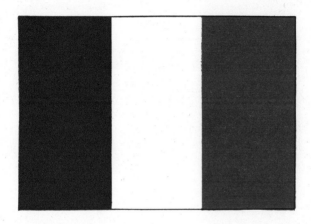

FRANCE

THE NATIONAL FLAG of France, the tricolor, was introduced in 1789 during the French Revolution. The order of the colors then was red, white, and blue. In 1830, the flag was changed to its present form with the blue next to the hoist.

The origin of the tricolor has been explained in various ways. According to history, after the fall of the Bastille, King Louis XVI realized that the new local government of Paris was one to be reckoned with and that the people of France were in sympathy with the National Assembly in Paris and not with the King and the Royalists. Late in 1789, he reorganized the government of Paris and approved the appointment of Lafayette as Commander of the National Guard. It is said that King Louis XVI came to Paris wearing a cockade of red, white, and blue, the red and blue being the colors of the arms of the city of Paris and the white the color of the House of Bourbon. Another account tells us that the national tricolor may be attributed to the blue Chape de Martin that Clovis carried, the red oriflamme (flag) of St. Denis, and the white flag that the Huguenots adopted.

FLAG OF THE GERMAN
REPUBLIC

FLAG OF THE GERMAN
REICH

GERMANY

THE NATIONAL FLAG of Germany, containing a black left-handed swastika, was adopted in 1933. Between 1919 when the Weimar Constitution was adopted and 1933, the national flag of Germany while she was a Republic was a tricolor. The black, red and gold flag had been used earlier in 1813 by General Von Lutzow and his men. Again, in 1848, it was used during the Revolution. Several university students, unions and groups also have used these colors. When the Nazi party came into power, the Nazi flag with the swastika was officially adopted as the national flag.

This later flag has the same colors as the earlier flag but the design is different. Black and white are the colors emblematic of Prussia and the colors that have been carried by the Hohenzollerns for more than five centuries. Three members of the Hohenzollerns, the ruling house of Prussia, have been emperors of Germany, the last being the Kaiser who abdicated in World War I. The red represents the old Hansa, the league to which many of the northern parts of Europe belonged.

The Hakenkreuz, as the swastika flag is called, contains the colors of the Reich. The interpretation the government placed upon the colors was that red and white were symbolic of the nation's strength in commerce, while black and white symbolized the armed might on which they felt prosperity depended.

The swastika in the flag is an ancient symbol. It has been used by the Indians and various pagan tribes, and has frequently been adopted as the symbol for the sun. The right-handed swastika is supposed to be the symbol of good luck and good omen; the left-handed swastika, on the other hand, has been the symbol of evil and darkness throughout the ages, and of the Nazis in our time.

GREAT BRITAIN

THE NATIONAL FLAG of Great Britain is a combination of the crosses of St. George, St. Andrew, and St. Patrick. The original national banner of England had the cross of St. George, its patron saint. In 1706, the flag was altered and the crosses of St. George and St. Andrew, who was the patron saint of Scotland, were conjoined. By a proclamation issued in 1801, the flag was again altered to show union with Ireland. The Cross of St. Patrick, the patron saint of Ireland, was added.

The Union Flag of 1801 is the same flag that is used today. Its red cross is that of St. George and both the white cross of St. Andrew and the red cross of St. Patrick are counterchanged.

Red, white, and blue ensigns are in use in Great Britain. From a document of Pepys dated 1867—he was then Secretary of the Admiralty—we learn that the British Fleet was divided into red, white, and blue squadrons. Lord Nelson thought this arrangement was confusing and ordered the entire fleet to use a white flag with the union in the canton. This is one of the flags referred to as union jacks. In 1864, the division of the fleet into red, white, and blue squadrons was ordered discontinued. The white ensign was thenceforth reserved for all British men of war, the blue ensign for vessels commanded by and manned by British Naval Reserve officers, and the red ensigns for all British merchant vessels.

The blue ensign is the flag that is used by British dependencies and self-ruling nations comprising the British Commonwealth of Nations. Frequently, the coat of arms or emblem of the country has been added, as in the case of Australia and of Canada.

GREECE

THE FIRST national flag of Greece, adopted in 1822, had a white cross on a red field. Ten years later the flag consisted of four blue stripes and five white ones. Later, in 1833, Otto of Bavaria ascended the throne of Greece. Though the colors in his arms, light blue and white, coincide with the colors in the Greek flag, they do not account for them. In 1863, Greece came under the influence of Denmark, at which time the light blue in the flag was changed to dark blue. A little later, the light blue was restored and it has remained to the present day.

The colors in the national flag originated in the War of Greek Independence of 1821. A group of Klephts battled Turkish forces near a monastery. The monks joined the fight and, as they were advancing, it occurred to them that they did not have a banner or flag. One man proffered his white foustanella, which is the white pleated skirt that is worn by the Evzones today, while another, a monk, removed his blue underrobe. Together, the white and blue colors were raised. This incident was the inspiration for the selection of the colors of the Greek flag.

The white stands for peace and purity, the blue for truth and loyalty. The cross appears in the canton because of the part played by the Church toward the achievement of Greece's independence from the Ottoman Empire. The nine white and blue stripes represent the nine syllables in the Greek phrase "eleutheria a thanatos," which means "liberty or death."

GUATEMALA

GUATEMALA WAS PART of the territory conquered by Spain in 1522 and remained part of Spain's colonial possessions in America until 1821, when she gained her independence. One year later, she voluntarily joined herself with Iturbide's Mexican Empire, but the Empire was short-lived. In 1823, Guatemala became a member of the Central American Federation and used its horizontally striped blue, white, and blue flag.

The first flag to be adopted by Guatemala after becoming a free state—a flag of seven horizontal stripes of blue, white, red, yellow, red, white, and blue—was authorized on March 14, 1851.

The Revolution of 1871 brought a change in the flag. On August 17th of that year, the Guatemalan Congress approved the flag that appears above. The flag is similar to the one used by Guatemala in 1823.

The colors in the flag have been interpreted in two ways. The first is that the white signifies peace, the blue the oceans, and the position of the white between the blue is intended to signify peace between the nations on either side of the ocean. A second meaning is that the blue stands for the sky and that the white stands for purity.

The coat of arms in the flag was also adopted in 1871. Inscribed on the parchment is "15 de setiembre de 1821," the date of the Guatemalan declaration of independence. The rifles and swords symbolize peace. That beautifully colored bird perched above the scroll is a Quetzal, national bird of Guatemala. It is the symbol of self-government and liberty, for the Quetzal is a bird of freedom. It is unable to live in captivity even when captured very young. Durability of the civic virtues and the national institutions are represented by the oak leaves, triumph and glory by the laurel leaves.

HAITI

HAITI WAS EXPLORED and first ruled by Spaniards. During these years Negro slaves were transported there and to this day its population is predominantly Negro. By a treaty signed in 1677, Spain was compelled to relinquish Haiti to the French.

The war for independence between the Haitians and the French began in the first years of the nineteenth century. Strangely enough, both sides were using the French tricolor. The confusion that resulted prompted General Dessalines to meet with other Haitian generals for the purpose of creating a flag. They met at Arcahaye on May 18, 1803. General Dessalines suppressed the white of the French tricolor, since white denotes peace and goodwill, and formed the Haitian flag out of the remaining two colors. The red represented the mulattoes, the blue the Negroes.

In 1807, during the secession from France, Jean Christophe replaced the blue in the flag with black, but this flag was not kept. The coat of arms was added to the flag by President Pétion, who assumed office in 1807. When Haiti became a republic in 1843, the government adopted the blue and red flag with coat of arms.

The palm tree in the arms stands for pride. Above it is a Phrygian cap, symbol of liberty. The trophy of arms, cannons, bayonets, flags, and drum is symbolic of Haitian independence achieved by arduous struggle. The motto of Haiti on the scroll, "L'Union Fait La Force," means "Union makes strength."

HONDURAS

Honduras was visited by Columbus in 1502. He landed at a place near what is now known as Cape Honduras. Settlement of the country began a few years later when a Spanish soldier of fortune set up a government. He was succeeded by Spanish rule after Cortez, coming down from Mexico, claimed the country for Spain.

Honduras was freed from the Spanish yoke at the same time as were some of the other Latin American countries. She declared her independence on September 15, 1821. Then, for a period of two years, Honduras was allied with the Mexican Empire, an arrangement that continued until the Central American Federation was established in 1823.

Upon the dissolution of the Federation in 1838, Honduras continued to use the Federation flag as her own. A new national flag was decided upon and adopted on February 16, 1866. This flag retains the colors of the earlier flag, a not uncommon occurrence, but the significance of the colors in the different countries that conserved them is not always alike. To Hondurans, the two blue stripes stand for the Atlantic and Pacific Oceans, the white for land—Honduras.

The five blue stars in the center of the flag represent the five states of Central America that composed the Central American Federation. In memory of them, Honduras placed the stars in her flag.

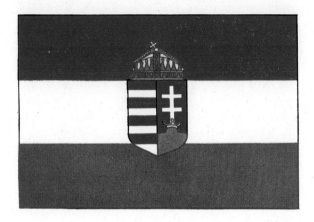

HUNGARY

THE NATIONAL FLAG of Hungary, as we see it today, is like the flag that was in use before Austria and Hungary were united. The flag of Austria-Hungary combined the colors and coats of arms of the two countries. After World War I, the boundary line drawn by the Treaty of Trianon in 1920 divided former Austria-Hungary into three nations: Austria, Hungary, and Czechoslovakia. Hungary resumed the flag that it had had in earlier times. •

The colors of the national flag were taken from the Hungarian coat of arms. The original arms date back to 1202, at which time the colors were red and white; in the seventeenth century, green was added to them.

The four white bands on the right side of the shield represent the four chief rivers of Hungary: the Danube, Theiss or Tisze, the Drava, and the Sava. The three green hills on the left side represent Hungarian mountains: the Tatra, Matra, and Fatra. Surmounting the center hill is a crown above which there is a double cross representing Christianity.

There is a legend concerning the curious angle at which the cross rests on the crown. This is not to be confused with the cross that appears on the left side of the shield. It is reported that thieves once stole the crown and tried to hide it in an iron casket. The casket was too shallow so they forced the crown bearing the cross down into it by pressing on the lid, thus bending the cross.

The cross was given to King Stephen of Hungary by Pope Sylvester II because Stephen was responsible for the conversion of the Magyars to Christianity. The Pope granted King Stephen the royal crown and conferred on him the right to have the cross borne before him at all times, the cross being the symbol of the apostolic power that was given to him.

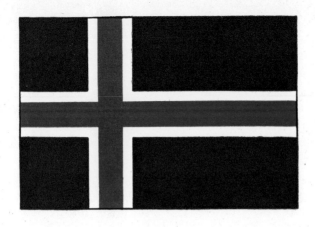

ICELAND

ICELAND WAS DISCOVERED in the ninth century by the Norse-men. In 1262, Iceland was under Norwegian rule. Then, in 1380, she came under Danish rule, and continued to be ruled by Denmark until the present century. Only recently, in 1941, did she cancel her union with Denmark and declare her independence. The parliament of Iceland is called the Althing. It is the oldest legislative body in existence; it has convened regularly, except for a very brief period, since the tenth century.

On November 22, 1913, Iceland was granted the right to have a flag of her own and created the flag she uses today. On June 19, 1915, the flag was approved by a Danish Royal De-cree. In 1918, Denmark recognized Iceland as a sovereign state, on condition that the King of Denmark would continue to be King of Iceland, too. As a sovereign state, Iceland con-tinued to use the flag chosen earlier and King Christian X gave his formal approval to the flag on February 12, 1919.

From olden times, Iceland has regarded blue and silver as her national colors. The arms of one of her leading families consisted of a silvery falcon on a blue shield. This emblem was taken as the seal of Iceland and later as the royal arms.

Christianity is the state religion of Iceland; therefore, the cross in the flag. Because the white cross on a blue background conflicted with the Greek flag, a red cross was superimposed, thus making the flag of Iceland a counterpart of the Norwegian flag.

In July, 1944, a law removed the crown from the arms, in keeping with Iceland's change to a republican form of government.

INDIA

INDIA IS ONE of the largest and most important of the countries under the British Crown, which together are loosely associated in what is known as the British Commonwealth and Empire. The British King is also Emperor of India. Nearly half the area of India is not British territory. Indian India is comprised of five hundred and sixty-two states ruled by semi-independent Princes and Chiefs in relations with the Crown. The Indian states each have flags.

The flag of British India is the Union Jack with the badge of India in the center. India's badge consists of the Star of India, a reproduction of the badge worn by those who have been admitted to the Order of the Star of India, which was established in 1861 by Queen Victoria. In addition to the motto and the star, there is a full sun in the badge. The rays of the sun symbolize royal authority. The flag that distinguishes the British Viceroy has an imperial crown surmounting the sun.

Equally well known as the flag of India is the flag of the Indian Merchant Marine. It is the blue ensign with the Union Jack in the canton. In the fly of the flag is placed the Star of India, too, but it is not ensigned by the crown.

IRAN

IRAN IS THE NAME of the country formerly known as Persia. When the country was called Persia, the flag consisted of three stripes of pale green, white, and pink, and these two pastel colors made the flag unique. No other nation has used pink in its flag.

About four hundred years ago, Persia adopted a flag on which appeared a lion couchant and a sun. In the eighteenth century, one imperial banner bore three crescents and another was embellished with three lions rampant. The nineteenth century witnessed the inception of the Persian tricolor, which bore a lion, a sun, and a scimitar. The present flag evolved from that. It was officially established in 1933.

The national flag of Iran when flown by the people is the plain tricolor. Whenever the national flag is flown from a government building, it must have the lion and sun motif on the white stripe. The green in the flag symbolizes the Mohammedan faith, the white peace, and the red courage and sacrifice.

The Red Cross organization in all Moslem countries is known as the Red Crescent Society, since followers of Mohammed cannot use the cross as their symbol. Seven of the eight Moslem countries Afghanistan, Egypt, Ethiopia, Iraq, Saudi Arabia, Syria and Turkey, use a red crescent on a white flag. Iran, however, uses the lion and sun emblem on a white flag.

IRAQ

IRAQ, the territory between the Arabian desert and Iran, was formerly called Mesopotamia. Iraq is the Arabian name. The famous city of Baghdad, city of Caliphs, renowned for its oriental splendor, is the capital of Iraq.

After World War I, by the terms of the treaty of peace with Turkey in 1920, Iraq was made an independent state under mandate to Great Britain. In addition to the territory that comprised Mesopotamia before the war, three Turkish vilayets or political divisions, Basra, Baghdad, and Mosul, were acquired. After the treaty of 1920, the flag of Iraq was adopted. Under the terms of this treaty, Iraq was supposed to remain under mandate to Great Britain for twenty years but, in 1930, Great Britain by treaty renounced its mandatory rights. The predominant religion of Iraq is the religion of Islam, Mohammedanism.

The significance of the colors in the flag has been described variously. One explanation is that red symbolizes the blood of the country's enemies, green the fertility of its land, black the fate of its enemies, and white its own bravery and chivalrousness.

95

Another explanation is that the black represents the Abbasid caliphs, white the Umayyad caliphs and green the Fatemid caliphs. The red symbolizes the Hashemite family to which King Ghazi, who ruled until 1939, belonged. An earlier member of the Hashemite family is remembered for the revolt he led against Turkey.

The two stars have been explained as representing, on the one hand, the two races of Iraq—the Arabs and the Kurds—and, on the other, the two important rivers—the Tigris and Euphrates.

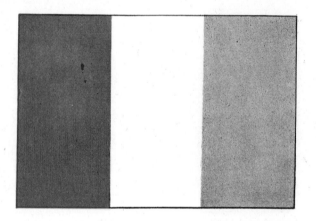

IRELAND

IRELAND INCLUDES Northern Ireland, also known as Ulster, and the Irish Free State, generally known by its Gaelic name, Eire. In 1922, the Irish Free State Act established a separate government for Eire. It is a member of the British Commonwealth of Nations and has the same status as Canada.

Eire formally adopted its tricolor in 1922, although the flag had been used earlier by a company of Irish volunteers who adopted it as their flag in 1914. The Home Rule Bill, giving Ireland its independence, was passed just as World War I broke and because of the war all action on it was delayed. The Irish volunteers, annoyed at the delay, staged the Easter Rebellion of 1916, at which time they used the tricolor.

The flag has a longer history as a symbol of the Irish fight for independence. A previous attempt to gain independence had been made in 1848 by a group known as The Young Ireland Movement. They, upon their return from France, brought back the green, white, and orange tricolor.

Green in the national flag of Eire represents the Catholics, orange the Protestants, and white the peace they desired to bring about.

ITALY

THE NATIONAL FLAG of Italy was established in 1861. A vertical tricolor of green, white, and red was used by an Italian legion under Napoleon in his First Italian Campaign of 1796. Some say that Napoleon designed it. When, in 1805, Italy was made a kingdom by Napoleon, the tricolor was used, but it was withdrawn upon the downfall of Napoleon in 1815.

In 1831, this same tricolor was hoisted by the liberals in the Papal States as a symbol of Italian nationalism and in rebellion against Metternich, the Austrian statesman, who ruled the kingdom. Seventeen years later, the nationalists again raised the tricolor while driving the Austrians from their land. The King of Sardinia adopted the tricolor as the flag of his kingdom in that same year, 1848.

In the meantime, while the tricolor had been in disuse, Mexico had adopted a flag that was identical. Upon readopting it, as it were, Italy asked that Mexico change her flag. As a compromise, each nation charged the center stripe of its flag with a distinctive emblem.

The King of Sardinia, a member of the House of Savoy,

charged the tricolor with his arms. The white cross, on the red ground, had been on the arms of members of the House of Savoy ever since 1315 when it was granted to Amadeus V, Duke of Savoy, by the Sovereign Order of St. John of Jerusalem for his assistance in defending their island, Rhodes, against the Saracens.

The Kingdom of Sardinia was the nucleus of modern Italy. In 1861, the King of Sardinia and his flag became the flag of a united Italy. There is another explanation for the colors in the flag, namely, that the red and white stand for the colors of the Royal House of Savoy and that green is the color of hope and symbolizes the hope for a United Italy. But as this explanation is ex post facto, the first interpretation is more credible.

JAPAN

THE JAPANESE call their land Nippon, derived from the words Nitsu, sun, and Phon, the rising. The name, Japan, is a corruption of the Chinese word Zapangn, which means source of the sun. Japan was so named by China because she lay west of Japan and thought of Japan as the source of the sun.

The Japanese have had a flag with a sun on it since the eighth century, but it has not always been designed as it is today. The present flag was adopted in 1859.

There are various interpretations of the sun on the flag. One is that the sun is the image of the Imperial ancestor, the sun goddess. Another is that the rising sun, or sunburst as it is sometimes termed, was chosen because Japan thought of herself as the place where the sun first appears and considered this an omen symbolic of Japan's position in the Orient. She interpreted it to mean that she was first and foremost the rising power in the East. The red in the flag symbolizes enthusiasm, the white patriotism.

LATVIA

LATVIA BECAME A REPUBLIC on November 18, 1918. From 1158 to 1549, Latvia or Lettland, the land of the Letts, was ruled by the Teutonic knights. Poland held sway until 1629, Sweden until 1721, the Russian Empire until 1918, and in that year Latvia proclaimed her independence.

The national flag of Latvia was in use in the thirteenth century. According to one account, the Teutonic knights or "Missionaries of the mailed fist" as they were referred to, occupied a castle in Cesis against a tribe of Zemgli. The Letts came to the assistance of the knights, carrying a banner of this design. The Letts themselves were conquered by the Teutonic knights who ruled over them for four hundred years, during which time they were serfs. They first acquired personal freedom in 1817. In 1905, they staged an unsuccessful insurrection for national freedom.

The Letts used the juice of berries to make the crimson for their original flag. Latvian poets say that the red in the flag indicates the readiness of the Latvians to give blood of their hearts for their freedom, which was represented by the white in the flag.

LIBERIA

LIBERIA IS a Negro republic situated on the western coast of Africa. The national flag resembles the flag of the United States. Through the efforts of the American Colonization Society, a group of freed Negroes emigrated to found the colony in 1822. President Monroe was in office at the time, and the capital of Liberia, Monrovia, is named for him. All the inhabitants of Liberia are of the African race.

In 1847, Liberia was declared a republic. Its form of government was patterned after that of the United States. So, too, was its flag, hoisted that same year for the first time.

The three colors in the flag represent the three divisions of Liberia at the time the flag was adopted. The eleven stripes represent the eleven signers of the Liberian Declaration of Independence. The unique character of the Liberian Republic is symbolized by the single star, Liberia being the only sovereign Negro state in the world.

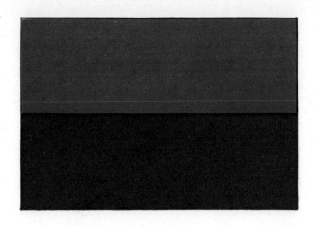

LIECHTENSTEIN

LIECHTENSTEIN IS ONE of the smallest independent principalities in Europe. In all, the country has an area of sixty-five square miles. It is situated between Austria and Switzerland.

The re ons for the choice of its colors, red and blue, are not defin ly known. The principality consists of two lordships, Scl enburg and Vaduz, which may account for them, since the colors in the shield of the ruling house have often been the source of flag colors.

The principality of Liechtenstein was founded in 1719. It was a member of the German Confederation until 1866. In the intervening years to the end of World War I, it was a dependency of Austria. On November 7, 1918, with the dissolution of Austria, Liechtenstein was made an independent principality.

The constitution of this country was established in 1921. It provides for a Diet of fifteen members who are elected by the people, all of whom have the right of suffrage. Liechtenstein is a hereditary monarchy, and Prince Franz Joseph II is the ruling monarch. Liechtenstein does not have any army or navy.

LITHUANIA

LITHUANIA, an ancient nation, was known as the Grand Principality of Lithuania in the thirteenth century. A wedding between the eighteen-year-old Queen of Poland and the young Duke of Lithuania in 1366 brought the two nations together.

In 1500, Lithuania and parts of Russia were united with Poland. For the next two hundred years, Lithuania was ruled by Poland. After Catherine the Great of Russia dismembered Poland in 1793, Lithuania became a part of the Russian Empire. Her independence was not achieved until the end of World War I.

Following the Declaration of Independence on February 16, 1918, a committee of Lithuanian artists met to choose the colors for the national flag. They decided to use those colors most popular in the folklore and songs of Lithuania.

The national flag was approved by the Lithuanian Constituent Assembly, which convened on May 15, 1920, in Kaunas, provisional capital of Lithuania. Its adoption in 1920 postdated the Treaty of Moscow, by which most of the great nations recognized the independence of Lithuania.

The yellow in the flag stands for the fields of ripening rye or wheat, symbolizing freedom from want; the green for the beautiful evergreen forests of Lithuania, symbolizing hope; and the red, "the most beautiful color" of flowers, for love of country.

LUXEMBOURG

THE NATIONAL FLAG of the Grand Duchy of Luxembourg began to be used in 1890, because for centuries Luxembourg had been under one or another of the larger European nations and was compelled to use the flag of these nations.

Luxembourg's colors first made their appearance in 1234. At that time, the seals used by the sons of the Countess of Ermesinde had a shield of silver and blue charged with a red lion. From these the national colors were derived.

The oldest known seal of Luxembourg is to be found affixed to the Charter of 1237. From the seal issues a ribbon of red, white, and blue. King John, the Blind, of Bohemia, gave the City of Luxembourg a charter granting it certain privileges. This charter of 1310 also had a seal with the same colors attached.

In 1814, Luxembourg was made a Grand Duchy and given to the King of Holland, who also bore the title of Grand Duke of Luxembourg. A part of the Grand Duchy was incorporated with Belgium in 1830. The remainder governed itself according to its Constitution. Under terms of the Treaty of London in 1867, Luxembourg was declared neutral territory and its independence was guaranteed.

The flag used by Luxembourg from 1814 to 1890 was the flag of the Netherlands. In 1890, the Grand Duchy's personal connection with the Netherlands was severed upon the death of King Wilhelm III of the Netherlands. Again, Luxembourg's very old flag was used.

MANCHUKUO

MANCHUKUO, formerly called Manchuria, was once a dependency of China, governed by a governor-general whom the Chinese Government appointed. Most of its inhabitants are Chinese. When China lost Manchuria to Japan, its name was changed to Manchukuo. Though it was listed as an independent state, it was actually in the possession of the Japanese.

The national flag of Manchukuo was adopted in 1932. There are two interpretations for its colors. The first is that yellow is the color of the Imperial House of the Emperor and his ancestors who have ruled the Chinese Empire. The red is there to represent enthusiasm, the blue youth, the white impartiality, and the black fortitude.

The second interpretation has to do with the various races of people who inhabit Manchukuo. Each color stands for one of the five chief races, namely: the Manchus, Mongolians, Koreans, Russians, and Chinese.

MEXICO

THE MEXICAN FLAG tells us much about the history of Mexico. Although it was adopted in 1821, the symbols represent events that occurred many hundreds of years before.

The Toltecs were the first to settle in Mexico, at the end of the seventh century. After four hundred years, they disappeared and the Aztecs, coming from the north, reached the shore of Lake Tezcoco in 1325. "There," according to legend, "they beheld, perched on the stem of a prickly pear, which shot out from the crevices of a rock that was washed by the waves, a royal eagle of extraordinary size and beauty, with a serpent in its talons, and his broad wings opened to the sun." The vision made them decide this was the site upon which they should build their city. These people developed into a strong nation before the Spanish conquered them.

Mexico won its independence from Spain in 1821, and the new nation began to think about a flag to represent itself. Three colors were chosen: the green, the color nearest the flagstaff, for independence, the white for purity of religion, and the red for the union of the Spanish element with the

Mexican nation. The Mexican coat of arms appears in the center of the white stripe. As was most appropriate, the coat of arms portrays the revelation of the early Aztecs—the eagle, perched on its left foot, upon a nopal (a cactaceous plant) growing from a rock in the water of the lake, with his right foot grasping a snake that he is in the act of tearing to pieces with his beak. Under this but part of it are two branches, one a laurel and the other an oak.

MONACO

Monaco is the smallest principality in Europe in size. It has an area of little more than seven square miles. Situated on the Mediterranean coast near Nice, Monaco is composed of the three communes of Monaco-Villa, La Condamine, and Monte Carlo. For eight hundred years, this smallest sovereign state has been independent.

From 968 until 1792 A.D., Monaco belonged to and was ruled by the princes of the House of Grimaldi. They were deposed at the time of the French Revolution. In 1814, the line of rulers was resumed. The coat of arms of the Prince of Monaco is a shield covered with red and white lozenges. The colors of the flag were taken from the arms.

Until 1911, Monaco was an absolute monarchy, but under the reigning Prince Albert a constitution was promulgated in that year. It provided for a national council of twelve members, elected for four years by the men of Monaco.

NETHERLANDS

THE NETHERLANDS FLAG is one of the oldest national ensigns. In 1354, the flag was red, white, and blue. These colors have flown from the masts of the Netherlands ships since that time.

In the sixteenth century, while the red, white, and blue ensign continued to be used by Netherlands merchantmen, another flag (the Prince-flag) of orange, white, and blue was adopted in honor of the Royal House of Orange, the ruling house of the Netherlands. Around this time, flags with nine, twelve, or more stripes, alternating red, white, and blue, were also in use as ensigns.

In the seventeenth century, during the years when the Republic of the United Netherlands had no Prince of Nassau as stadholder, the orange of the ensigns was made red. From 1817, when by royal decree the present flag of the Netherlands was adopted, the flag has consisted of three equal horizontal stripes of red, white, and blue.

The Vlaggelied or Dutch Flag Song describes the meaning of the flag. Here, in the second stanza, is the significance of its colors:

> Is not that Blue in its spotless splendor,
> Dedicated to the loyalty of our forebears?
> Does not that Red speak of their virility?
> And courage in so many battles.
> Or does not that White, so pure and mild,
> Point to the piety, that await the blessings from God?
> The blessings, which alone can satisfy!

NEWFOUNDLAND

NEWFOUNDLAND, the oldest British colony in terms of discovery, was first sighted by John Cabot in 1497. Cabot claimed the new land for King Henry the Seventh. By 1630, only about three hundred families inhabited the island, used as a fishing station by both the French and British, who quarreled frequently over their rights. Under the terms of the Treaty of Utrecht in 1713, the island was ceded to the British. A few years later the British appointed a governor. Newfoundland was granted the right to representative government in 1832.

The national flag, like that of all the British colonies, is the Union Jack which is the only flag supposed to be flown by British colonies on land. Certain British colonies, Newfoundland is one of them, were granted the right to fly the red ensign, with their coat of arms placed on the fly, from their merchant vessels. These flags are, more often than not, associated with the colony and used on occasions of a national character. The red ensign of Newfoundland has on the fly the Newfoundland badge, bearing the coat of arms that were approved in 1637.

In the badge, there is a representation of Mercury, the God of Commerce, presenting to Britannia a fisherman who in a kneeling position is offering her the harvest of the sea. Above is a scroll inscribed with the words "Terra Nova," meaning "New Earth," and below are the words "Haec tibi dona fero," meaning "I bring you these gifts."

NEW ZEALAND

NEW ZEALAND, situated about twelve hundred miles east of Australia, is an autonomous British Dominion. Discovered in 1642 by a Dutch explorer, Abel Tasman, and explored in 1769 by Captain James Cook, it was established as a colony under British sovereignty in 1840. In 1907, the colony of New Zealand was given Dominion status. It is governed by a governor-general, the general assembly, and a prime minister. Wellington is the capital of New Zealand.

The national flag of New Zealand is the Union Jack officially. According to British flag law, all dominions, colonies, and dependencies of the British Empire are supposed to use the Union Jack as the national flag on land. In practice, however, the red or blue ensigns on which the dominions and colonies have been granted the right to place their arms or badges, for use at sea, are most frequently thought of as the national flag and are used on national occasions. The blue ensign of New Zealand, with four white-bordered red stars in the form of the constellation of the Southern Cross, was first used at the beginning of this century. The red ensign with four white stars in the same position is used by the New Zealand merchant marine.

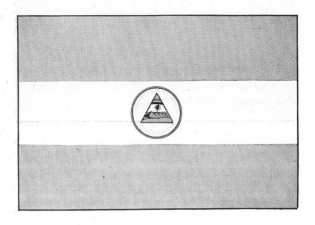

NICARAGUA

NICARAGUA IS NAMED after an Indian chief. Davilla, a Spaniard, discovered the country in 1522. Spanish rule prevailed here, as it did in so many other Latin American countries, until 1821. Nicaragua and the four other Central American countries, upon securing their independence, formed a Central Committee. For the next two years, in agreement with the decision of the Committee, Nicaragua and her sister nations joined with Iturbide's Mexican Empire.

In 1823 Iturbide fell and the Mexican Empire was dissolved, and the five Central American nations declared their independence. They formed a Federation, which lasted until 1838 when it was dissolved. Subsequently, the republics each chose a flag of their own.

Nicaragua adopted in 1854 a flag of white, yellow, and scarlet. This flag was used for a time, but it was decided to replace it with the flag of 1823. Because Nicaragua looked forward to the reunion of the five Central American nations into one political entity, Nicaragua passed a law in 1908 approving a new flag and coat of arms, symbols that were felt to be better adapted to its peoples, but the national flag of Nicaragua retains the colors used by the Central American Federation.

The coat of arms in the center stripe contains a triangular device that portrays Nicaragua's "aspiration for rebirth of the political entity which was formed by the five states." The equilateral triangle is a symbol of three principles essential in government: right, justice, and truth. The five Central American nations are represented by the five volcanoes of Central America. A Phrygian cap represents liberty and the rainbow symbolizes peace. Around the circle that encloses the triangle are inscribed the words "Republica de Nicaragua, America Central" meaning "Republic of Nicaragua, Central America."

NORWAY

NORWAY IN THE EARLY period of its history was a monarchy. In 1397, Queen Wilhelmina of Denmark succeeded to the throne and by the Union of Calmar united the kingdoms of Norway, Denmark, and Sweden. The union lasted about four centuries. A strong nationalist sentiment developed in Norway in the latter part of the eighteenth century.

In May, 1814, the Norwegians declared their independence and adopted a constitution. They offered the crown to the Danish Crown Prince. Sweden intervened and a compromise was effected. The national assembly of Norway negotiated a treaty whereby Norway was to be a "free, independent and indivisible kingdom, united with Sweden under one king." The union was not entirely satisfactory and, in 1905, Norway declared itself completely independent.

Flags with crosses have a very old tradition in Scandinavia. St. Olav, who died in 1030, used a yellow cross on a red background. Until 1814, Norway had the same flag as Denmark. For the next seven years, it used the flag of Denmark charged with the Norwegian national arms. Then in 1821 the flag that is currently flown was adopted. For a brief period between 1844 and 1898, when Norway and Sweden were united, this flag was used with the Swedish Norwegian Union mark in the corner. In 1898, Norway reverted to the flag adopted in 1821.

The flag of Norway is composed of the old Dannebrog (Danish flag) with a blue cross added to indicate independence. A poetic interpretation of the colors is given in song: red represents the blood of the heart, white the snow, and blue the fields and oceans.

PANAMA

PANAMA IS THE YOUNGEST of the Central American republics. Its name is an Indian word meaning abounding in fish. Panama is bathed by the waters of the Caribbean on the north and the Pacific Ocean on the south. Balboa forced his way through the jungles of Panama and discovered the Pacific Ocean in 1513. From then until 1821, Panama was a Spanish colony. She declared her independence in 1821 and joined Greater Colombia of her own volition. The next eighty years witnessed numerous movements toward separation, the Liberal and Conservative parties unable to agree, but Panama did not separate from Colombia until 1903, the year she obtained her independence with the help of the United States.

The national flag of Panama was adopted in 1903. The red quarter and star symbolizes the Liberal Party, the blue quarter and star the Conservative Party, and the white quarters the unity it was hoped the parties would achieve. Red in the flag also symbolizes liberty and blue, faith. The stars are the symbols of sovereignty.

The separatist movement that finally effected Panamanian independence was led by Dr. Manuel Amador. His son, Senor Manuel Amador, Jr., is supposed to have designed the flag for the new republic and his mother, is said to have made the first flag. There is some evidence that a Madame Bunau-Varilla, wife of the Panamanian representative was the true Betsy Ross of Panama.

PARAGUAY

PARAGUAY WAS SETTLED by the Spanish at Asuncion in 1536, and remained under Spanish rule until 1811. Jose Francia, secretary of the Junta, a revolutionary movement, took the government in his hands in that year. Through a bloodless revolution, Paraguay achieved its independence.

The first flag of Paraguay was adopted in 1811. It bore the coat of arms of the King of Spain. Some time later, the exact date is not known, the tricolor currently in use began to replace the flag of 1811. It was officially adopted on November 27, 1842.

The belief that Francia, who was President of Paraguay from 1816 to 1840, had something to do with the design of the flag is well founded for he was a great admirer of Napoleon and the colors of this flag are the same as the French tricolor. Note that the national arms of Paraguay, consisting of a star and palm and olive branches, also came into existence in Francia's time and that the star is reminiscent of Napoleon's Star of Destiny.

The red in the flag signifies war, the white peace, and the blue order. A star and palm and olive branches constitute the national symbol. The national flag of Paraguay is unique in that it is the only national flag to have one side different from the other. The reverse side of the flag has the seal of the treasury (Hacienda); the national coat of arms is on the obverse. In the seal on the reverse are the lion, symbol of finance; the Phyrgian cap, symbol of liberty; and "Paz y Justicia," an inscription that means "Peace and Justice."

PERU

THE NATIONAL FLAG of Peru was adopted by the Peruvian Congress on February 25, 1825, and has been in constant use since that time. It was preceded by two other flags that played an important part in Peru's fight for freedom.

San Martín and his patriot army landed in what is now known as Independence Bay in 1820. The Spanish flag that flew there seemed to him wholly incompatible with what he was fighting to accomplish. On October 21, 1820, he issued a decree establishing a new flag for Peru. It was to be divided diagonally with the upper and lower triangles white and the lateral ones red. In the center, there was to appear a coat of arms also designed by him. This flag was raised in

Lima on July 28, 1821, when San Martín proclaimed the independence of Peru. Actually, the liberation of Peru was accomplished a few years later by Bolívar and Sucre after their defeat of the Spanish forces at the battles of Junin and Ayacucho.

As the flag of San Martín was difficult to construct and further was of a provisional character only, a new flag was approved by Marshal Torre Tagle on March 15, 1822. This flag was replaced, in 1825, by the flag that Peru now has. All three flags, though different in design, were alike in color. The red in the flag symbolizes the blood of the patriots, the white right and justice.

The coat of arms was also adopted in 1825. A llama in the first quarter of the shield is symbolic of Peru's wealth in the animal kingdom, a cinchona tree in the second quarter symbolizes her wealth in the vegetable kingdom, and the cornucopia in the lower half, out of which pour coins of gold, is the symbol of her mineral wealth.

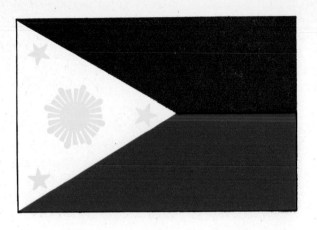

THE PHILIPPINES

THE PHILIPPINES were discovered in 1521 by the Portuguese explorer, Magellan. He named the archipelago St. Lazarus. The Spanish annexed the islands in 1542 and renamed them Philippine after Crown Prince Philip, later King Philip II.

Objection to Spanish rule grew steadily. Two years before the Spanish-American War, dissatisfaction was so great that the Filipinos revolted. The Insurgents carried the flag shown above. It was called the Kapitunan flag, meaning Insurgents' flag. At the close of the Spanish-American War, a treaty provided for the cession of the Philippines to the United States. Since that time, the Philippines have flown the American flag.

In 1935, President Roosevelt issued a proclamation that promised the Filipinos their independence in 1946 and permitted the people to elect their officials by ballot immediately. The first president of the Philippines was inaugurated on November 14, 1935. One of his first acts was officially to establish the design of the Philippine flag in March, 1936.

Although under the United States, the Philippines have used the flag of the Kapitunan since 1920. At present, it is always flown next to the flag of the United States. However, it will probably be sanctioned as the Philippine national flag when independence is declared.

The red in the flag stands for courage, the white for purity, and the blue for hope. Symbolic of unity is the sun, whose eight rays represent the first eight provinces that revolted against Spain. The stars represent the three great geographical divisions, Luzon, Visayan, and Mindanao.

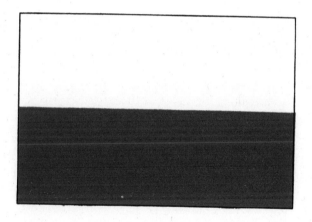

POLAND

POLAND, a republic since 1918, had its national beginnings in the tenth century. It was then a military state ruled by a king. In the fourteenth century it rose to be a great power and continued to be until the eighteenth century. In 1386, the Queen of Poland married the Duke of Lithuania and brought the two countries together. In the 1780's Poland was partitioned, again in 1792, and finally, in 1795, she ceased to exist as an independent state.

Despite the fact that Poland had not existed for well over a century as a nation, strong feelings of Polish nationalism united the Poles in their desire for recreation of the Polish state. At the end of World War I, Poland's independence was declared. The Treaty of Versailles recognized the new republic in 1919.

The Republic of Poland adopted a flag of red and white. According to legend, Lechonce, one of the ancestors of the first Polish ruler, found in a rocky vastness a white eagle's nest. Against the red glowing evening sun these eagles seemed to have a symbolic significance for him and his family.

The first dynasty of Polish kings, the Piasts, adopted the white eagle in a red field as their coat of arms. The emblem was later taken over by the dynasty of the Jagellons, though they introduced certain changes in the form of the eagle. Later, when the national emblem and the royal coat of arms were established, white and red were adopted as the Polish national colors.

The interpretation that has been placed upon the colors is that white denotes peace, and red denotes liberty.

PORTUGAL

PORTUGAL HAS BEEN an independent state since 1139. To trace the beginnings of Portugal, we must go back to King Ferdinand of Castile and Leon who had a son, Alfonso VI of Leon. Alfonso's daughter married Count Henry of Burgundy. She was given, as her dowry, the counties of Coimbra and Oporto, which entitled Count Henry to the title of Count of Portugal.

The son of Count Henry took control of the government in 1128 and revolted against Castile. He declared the independence of Portugal and set up a kingdom of his own. Portugal continued to be a monarchy until 1910, when a revolution overthrew the king and Portugal was proclaimed a republic. Prior to the revolution, the flag of Portugal was half blue and half white.

The national flag of Portugal shown above was created in 1910 after the revolution. The arms in the flag are not new. They date back to 1139, when Alfonso of Portugal defeated five Moorish princes and, to commemorate his victory, adopted a coat of arms bearing five blue shields with five white circles, the latter symbolizing the five wounds of Christ through whose intervention Alfonso believed he was able to overcome the Moorish infidels. The red border was added to the arms in 1254 by Alfonso III upon his marriage to the daughter of the King of Castile. In memory of Prince Henry, commonly called Prince Henry the Navigator because of his great interest in and assistance to the science of navigation, the armillary sphere was added to the arms when the flag was designed in 1910.

The green in the flag is a further tribute to Prince Henry, who was made a Knight of St. Benedict. The cross and ribbon of these knights were green. The red was adopted as the color of the republic and is the color symbolic of revolution.

RUMANIA

RUMANIA IS SOMETIMES said to have been settled by the Romans in the second century A.D. hence, the other spelling of the name, Romania—but historians generally agree that the original settlers of Rumania were nomads who poured out of Asia into Europe. From the sixteenth century on, Rumania consisted of the two states of Wallachia and Moldavia, which were under the suzerainty of Turkey. In 1856, they declared their independence. At the end of World War I, with the reapportionment of the Balkan states, Rumania emerged a much larger state than she had ever been.

The national flag of Rumania was adopted in 1859, although it was first used during the revolutionary period of 1848. The blue in the flag represents the sky, the gold the country's wealth, and the red the nation's bravery. The royal arms that appear in the center stripe bear a shield that is quartered. The shield contains the arms of the territories that comprise Rumania. The first quarter, a displayed eagle, represents Wallachia; the second quarter, a bull's head, Moldavia; the third quarter, a lion rampant on a bridge, Banat; and the fourth quarter, an eagle over seven checkers (for seven castles), represents Transylvania (the German name for this place means seven cities). The base of the shield has two dolphins for Bessarabia. At the center, the escutcheon of pretense shows the Hohenzollern arms. Below the shield is the Rumanian motto "Nihil sine Deo," meaning "Nothing without God."

SAN MARINO

SAN MARINO IS THE SECOND smallest republic in the world. It embraces an area of thirty-eight square miles on the side of Mt. Titan in the Apennines near the Adriatic Sea. San Marino, as well as Switzerland, claims to be the oldest republic in the world.

San Marino was named after a missionary, Marinus, who settled on the slopes of Mt. Titan in the fourth century. Marinus was a stone cutter by trade. He came to supervise the rebuilding of the walls of Rimini, a city in Italy. When his work was done, he and his followers went up to the mountains to live. Before his death, Marinus gathered them around him and gave them the mountains on which they lived, free from other men. He urged them never to seek to enlarge their territory by war or violence. San Marino has managed to keep its independence and democratic institutions throughout sixteen centuries, heeding well the advice of Marinus, founder and patron saint.

The national flag of San Marino bears the coat of arms of San Marino, a pictorial representation of its geography and its government. The capital of San Marino is on top of a hill. It is surrounded by three rows of ramparts and three towers, which are depicted in the arms. These medieval towers are called Penne, meaning plumes, and the pun is carried out in the ostrich feathers that float from the towers. "Libertas," inscribed on the scroll, means independence but may refer also to Libertas, the Goddess of Liberty. Oak and laurel branches on either side of the shield are symbols of strength and glory.

SAUDI ARABIA

THE KINGDOM OF SAUDI ARABIA was created at the end of World War I. It combines the Sultanate of Nejd and the Kingdom of Hejaz, wherein are located the cities of Mecca and Medina, two very important cities in Mohammedan life. Mecca was the birthplace of Mohammed who founded the religion of Islam, and Medina is the city where Mohammed died and where his tomb rests enshrined by the Mosque of the Prophet. To these cities hundreds of Mohammedans annually make pilgrimages. So sacred are the cities that peoples of other faiths are not permitted to live in them.

Although the kingdom of Saudi Arabia came into being in 1918, the flag it uses is supposed to have been designed over a hundred years ago. The flag is almost square. Inscribed in Arabic on the flag is the motto of the Mohammedans, "There is no God but God, and Mohammed is the Prophet of God." The white scimitar below the inscription represents the militant quality of their faith.

The flag is green because green is the color sacred to Mohammedans. The story is that the Angel Gabriel gave Mohammed a green silk banner. The prophet used it as a curtain. Ayesha, his wife, tore it down and gave it to Mohammed to be the chief banner of Islam. This sacred banner, which the Turks have preserved, has on it a gold hand holding a copy of the Koran.

SOVIET UNION

THE SOVIET UNION, officially the Union of Soviet Socialist Republics, is another name for Russia. For several hundred years, Russia was ruled by Czars. One of these, Peter the Great, is said to have chosen the colors that appeared in the various flags of Russia, merchant and others. They were white, blue, and red. The flags were horizontal tricolors with the white stripe uppermost, blue in the middle, and red at the bottom.

As time went on, the rule of the Czars grew more and more oppressive. In 1917, the people revolted. Out of the revolutionary movement, the Communist government was established. The flag of the Communists became the flag of the Soviet Union.

The red in the flag was chosen because it is a symbol of revolution. It also is supposed to represent the common humanity of all peoples. The sickle and hammer, the emblem of Communism, represent the union of labor: the sickle for agricultural workers and the hammer for industrial workers. The red star is the symbol of the authority vested in the government of the Soviet Union.

There are at present sixteen Soviet republics, each of which has a flag of its own. The national flag and the flags of the republics are red. The state flags differ from the national flag of the Soviet Union only in the design in the canton.

SPAIN

THE FLAG of the Republic of Spain was established in 1936. The mural crown above the shield is indicative that Spain is no longer a monarchy. Before 1931, the shield of the Kingdom of Spain was ensigned by a royal crown.

The arms of Spain that appear in the flag trace the development of minor states into what became the Kingdom of Spain and later the Republic of Spain. For the story of these arms we must turn to the year 1031 when Navarre and Castile united. Navarre is represented by chains. Her arms appear in the fourth quarter of this shield. It is said that the

King of Navarre and his knights broke loose the chains defending the Almohede Sultan's tent, in battle with the Moors at Las Navas de Tolosa in 1213 A.D. From that time on the arms of the Kings of Navarre were emblazoned with the chain.

Castile means castle; the castle in the first quarter is the charge of this kingdom. Charges frequently had some resemblance to the name of the person or place they represented, either in meaning or sound. The Kingdom of Leon joined the Kingdoms of Navarre and Castile in 1037. Here, too, the arms are a symbolic translation of the name. The second quarter shows the lion, the arms of Leon.

When in 1474, Ferdinand II of Aragon married Isabella of Castile, the arms shown in the third quarter were added. They are the arms of Aragon, four red stripes on a gold background. According to legend, Geoffrey, Count of Barcelona, allied himself in battle with Prince Charles the Bald. The Count was wounded and Prince Charles, wishing to show him honor, dipped four fingers in his blood and ran them down the Count's shield. Aragon united with Barcelona soon after and adopted the arms of the Kingdom of Barcelona, which King Ferdinand inherited. Ferdinand conquered Granada in 1492 and the pomegranate, the arms of that kingdom, appears in the triangle at the base of the shield.

The Pillars of Hercules on either side of the shield represent Gibraltar and Tangier. At one time, the scroll that intertwines the pillars bore the motto "Ne Plus Ultra" which, translated literally, means "No more beyond." This was changed to "Plus Ultra" meaning "More beyond" after Columbus proved the earth was round and that there were other lands yet unknown and undiscovered.

The colors of the flag were chosen because they were the colors of the arms of King Ferdinand and though the design of the flag has been changed many times, these colors have been retained.

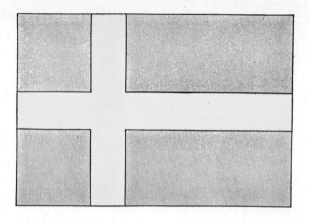

SWEDEN

SWEDEN IS A CONSTITUTIONAL MONARCHY, with a history that dates from 1000 A.D. Many legends have come down to us regarding events that preceded the year 1000 but they are not known to be authentic.

Queen Wilhelmina of Denmark succeeded to the throne in 1397. By the Union of Calmar, she joined the three Scandinavian countries, Norway, Denmark, and Sweden. This union was not popular with the people of Sweden and they determined to gain their independence. After many revolts they were finally, in 1523, successful. Sweden was separated from Norway and Denmark. Gustavus I Vasa, who had led the revolt, was made king.

The national flag of Sweden flown in 1523 in Gustavus I Vasa's reign had the blue field with a yellow cross that has continued in use ever since. In 1815, a law was passed establishing these colors as the colors of the national flag. The colors are said to have their origin in the crests of early Swedish kings. King Erik, the Saint, upon his return from the Crusades in 1157, instituted the cross used in the flag of Sweden thereafter.

From 1814 to 1905, Norway and Sweden were united under the Crown of Sweden. During this time, the union of the two countries was indicated by a combination of the colors of both flags in the canton. When Norway gained her independence in 1905, the colors in the upper corner of the flag were removed and Sweden's flag reverted to its earlier design.

SWITZERLAND

SWITZERLAND, with San Marino, claims to be the oldest republic in the world. Twenty-two cantons form the Swiss Confederation. In the reign of Charlemagne, Switzerland was part of the Frankish Empire. Upon his death, it fell under Austrian rule. In the thirteenth century, three forest cantons, Uri, Unterwalder, and Schwyz, united against their Austrian ruler, and defeated the Austrians at Morgarten in 1315. They carried a red banner with a white cross into battle.

Three other cantons, Lucerne, Zurich, and Berne joined

them and, in 1329, the forces marched against the Austrian nobles. They bore the "sign of the Holy Cross, a white cross on a red shield, for the reason that the freeing of the nation was for them a cause as sacred as the deliverance of the Holy Places."

In 1499, the Swiss fought the Austrians again, on the Rhine, and were victorious. Emperor Maximilian confirmed the liberties of the Swiss cantons, though it was not until the Peace of Westphalia in 1646 that Swiss independence was complete. The Federation of the Swiss cantons used the red flag with the white cross but it was not officially adopted as the national flag until 1840.

The major powers in Europe agreed in 1815 to guarantee Switzerland's neutrality. An International Conference was called to determine how best to care for the wounded in battle. The man behind this humanitarian cause was M. Jean Henri Dunant, a Swiss. The conference was held in Geneva in 1863 and chose as its emblem the Swiss flag with colors counterchanged. The Red Cross flag is a tribute to the Swiss for their work in founding the organization whose concern is care of the sick and wounded of war, whatever their color or creed, race or nationality.

SYRIA

SYRIA WAS proclaimed a republic on September 16, 1941. The majority of its population is Arabian and consequently Mohammedanism is the prevailing religion. Agriculture is the chief occupation of the people.

The national flag of republican Syria is the same flag that was first flown in Aleppo on January 1, 1932, and hoisted officially on June 11, 1932, in Damascus, when Syria was a French mandated territory. The flag flown on these two occasions, in turn, was patterned after a flag flown by King Feisal upon his ascension to the throne in 1920, called the Hashemite banner.

The green stripe in the flag stands for the Omayyad caliphates, the white for the Abbaside dynasty, and the black for the early Islamic era. The three vilayets (political districts) of Damascus, Aleppo, and Deir ez Zor are represented by the three stars.

THAILAND

Thailand was known as Siam until recently. In 1939, it restored its ancient name, Thailand (Muang Thai). Siamese, Laos, Chinese, Malays, and Cambodians compose the population. The people are interested primarily in agriculture and are good farmers. Buddhism, a reformed version of Brahmanism, is the religion of the Siamese and Laos, who constitute the majority of the population. Transmigration of the soul is a basic tenet of this religion.

The national flag established in 1899 consisted of a red field with a white elephant in the center. Xacca was the founder of the Siamese nation. His mother is supposed to have dreamt that she gave birth to a white elephant. This led the Brahmans to believe that after eighty thousand migrations, Xacca became a white elephant. The field of the flag was red because red is the color sacred to Brahma, the creator of Brahmanism.

The national flag of Thailand was changed in 1917. The flag is like the former merchant flag except for the blue stripe in the center. This was added in 1927 by King Rama

138

VI because blue was the color of Siamese Navy flags. The flag is called the Trairanga flag.

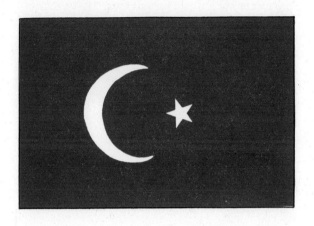

TURKEY

TURKEY WAS DECLARED a republic in October, 1923. The capital of Turkey, now, is Ankhara but for many centuries Constantinople was its capital. Constantinople in ancient times was called Byzantium, in modern times it is called Istambul.

The white crescent in the Turkish flag is sometimes attributed to an event that occurred in 339 B.C. According to legend, the Macedonian Emperor, Philip of Macedon, besieged Byzantium but encountered difficulty. He determined to undermine the walls by night. A crescent moon enabled the Byzantines to discover Emperor Philip and his warriors and to save their city.

The Byzantines, thereupon, chose the crescent moon for the badge of their city and erected a statue to their patroness,

Diana, goddess of the moon. In 1453, Byzantium fell to the Turks. They adopted the crescent moon for their symbol and placed it on a red flag, signifying that Constantinople had been gained on a field of blood. But there is another explanation. It is said that Ertkul, father of Ottoman, had a dream in which a half moon arose from the lap of Edebai, the Saracen prophet, and that thereafter the Ottomans decided to use the half moon in their flag. The star represents the morning star Al Tarek which is exceedingly bright.

The Turkish flag has undergone many changes. Sometimes it had had one crescent, sometimes more. The influence of Turkey's flag upon the flag of Egypt is apparent. Its influence on the flag of other Mohammedan countries in this and preceding centuries is no less apparent.

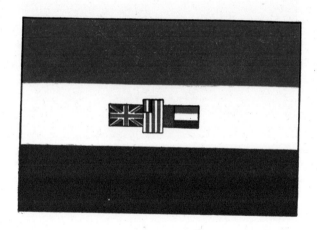

UNION OF SOUTH AFRICA

THE UNION OF SOUTH AFRICA is composed of the colonies of the Cape of Good Hope, Natal, the Transvaal, and the Orange Free State, and was formed in 1909. It has the status of a dominion within the British Commonwealth of Nations.

Cape Colony, the first of the provinces to be colonized, was settled by the Dutch in 1652. With the discovery of great mineral wealth, more and more people arrived, many of them British. The Boers, as the Dutch were called, moved into Natal, the Transvaal, and the Orange Free State. Conflict arose between Great Britain and the Boers and in 1899 war was declared. Peace was made in 1902, and all the Boers became British subjects. Seven years later the colonies were united into the Union of South Africa.

The flag flown was the blue ensign of Great Britain with the coat of arms of the Union of South Africa in the fly. But, in 1927, the Union of South Africa, contrary to the rule established for dominions of the British Empire, decided to design a flag of its own. The flag was severely objected to at first but was finally approved and adopted through the passing of a special Union Nationality and Flag Act. The Union Jack and the flag of the Union of South Africa are flown together on government buildings; both are required to be of equal size and are hoisted and lowered simultaneously.

The colors of the national flag of the Union of South Africa are the orange, white, and blue of the old Dutch flag chosen because the Dutch first settled there. In the center are the Union Jack, the old flag of the Orange Free State, and the old Transvaal Vierkleur. Together these flags represent the provinces.

URUGUAY

THE NATIONAL FLAG of Uruguay evolved from the flag designed by José Gervasio Artigas, national hero of Uruguay, at the time he was fighting for Uruguay's independence. Artigas was an officer in the King's constabulary in Uruguay. After an argument with one of his superiors, he fled and offered his services to the opposition—that is, the patriots in Buenos Aires who were staging a revolt. The year was 1810. Their attempt to put an end to Spanish domination in the viceroyalty of the Rio de la Plata was only partially successful. Two of the provinces, Uruguay and Paraguay, had not joined forces with them.

The patriots welcomed Artigas. A year later, he and a small band of men returned to Uruguay for the purpose of overthrowing the Spanish governor at Montevideo. At Las Piedras, just north of Montevideo, Artigas and his men fought and defeated the King's Army. There, for the first time, the flag of Artigas was unfurled. It consisted of three stripes of blue, white, and blue, over which was a diagonal red bar.

In 1814, Spanish rule was definitely ended. Then, in 1817, Uruguay came under Portuguese rule. Artigas' pioneer efforts toward independence sowed the seed for another movement, the Treinta y Tres (The Thirty-Three). The work of this band of patriots led to the war for independence that began in 1825 and continued until 1828. Their flag consisted of three horizontal stripes of azure, white, and red.

In 1828, Uruguay achieved her independence and on December 16th of that year the Legislative Assembly passed an act establishing that the flag be white with nine azure stripes and that the canton have depicted on it a sun. This was modified on July 11, 1830, by an act approving the present design.

The nine stripes symbolize the nine political departments that form the Republic of Uruguay. The full blazing sun, known as El Sol de Mayo or Sun of May, symbolizes Uruguay's maturing into an independent nation.

VENEZUELA

VENEZUELA WAS DISCOVERED by Columbus in 1498. Vespuccius visited the land a year later, and, finding there a little Indian village built on stakes across Lake Maracaibo, he named it Venezuela, which means Little Venice. The country was colonized by the Spanish and belonged to Spain for three centuries.

In 1810, Simon Bolívar, a Venezuelan by birth but honored by many other South American countries for his great vision and achievements in bringing Spanish domination to an end, joined General Miranda's army of patriots. It was General Miranda's hope to free all the South American countries and to unite them into one state. With this in mind, as early as 1806, he designed a flag of yellow, blue, and red stripes to be used by a United South America. This was the flag used by General Miranda when he invaded Coro on the western coast of Venezuela.

Venezuela declared its independence in 1811 and raised the flag of General Miranda in Cathedral Square, Caracas, the capital city. Two years later, Bolívar's army and the Spanish army were again locked in combat, for Spain was eager to regain her possession. In 1821, Venezuela was finally freed. She united with New Granada to form the Republic of Greater Colombia. Venezuela seceded from the Republic in 1829 and became completely independent.

The colors in the Venezuelan flag mean that rich Venezuela, as symbolized by the gold, is separated from bloody Spain (red), by the blue ocean. Seven white stars forming a half moon were chosen to represent the seven provinces that constituted the Venezuelan Confederation at the time she declared her independence on July 5, 1811.

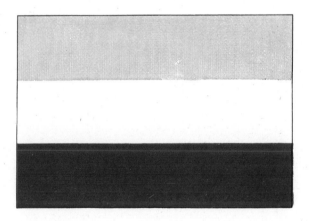

YUGOSLAVIA

THE KINGDOM OF YUGOSLAVIA was formed at the end of World War I. Yug means south and Yugoslavia is the union of the southern Slavs: the Serbs, Croats, and Slovenes. Because of their homogeneity, the six provinces of Croatia, Slovenia, Bosnia, Hertzegovina, Dalmatia, and Voyvodina and the states of Montenegro and Serbia voted to become one nation.

Serbia as an independent state had a flag consisting of three horizontal stripes of red, blue, and white. Montenegro's flag before World War I consisted of a red field with a white border and the royal arms in the center of the flag. Croatia's flag consisted of three horizontal stripes of red, white, and blue.

The national flag adopted on December 1, 1918, by the United Kingdom of Serbs, Croats, and Slovenes, as Yugoslavia was known at first, was decreed to be blue, white, and red because these colors had been the colors in the individual flags of the countries that were united. The stripes in the flag are arranged to make them appear different from the flags used by Serbia and Croatia.

The United Kingdom of Serbs, Croats, and Slovenes was proclaimed the Kingdom of Yugoslavia in 1929. The same flag was recognized to be the flag of the Kingdom of Yugoslavia.

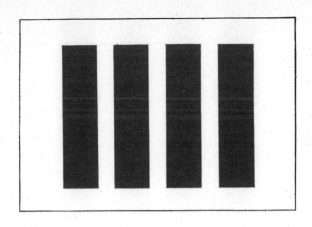

UNITED NATIONS FLAG OF
FOUR FREEDOMS

THE UNITED NATIONS FLAG of Four Freedoms came into being in 1942. It was designed by Brooks Harding, Director of the Four Freedoms Committee, in response to a need he recognized for a flag that could be flown second to the national flag and that yet would represent a country as being a member of the family of nations designated the United Nations. These nations, governed diversely, some democracies, some republics, some monarchies, nevertheless had united because of common agreement, nationally, on the inherent right of their citizens to four basic freedoms and, internationally, because of a common purpose to maintain law and order in the world.

The flag, while simple in design, is pregnant with meaning. Its white background stands for peace and purity, its red for the blood dedicated to the cause of freedom. The four upright bars represent the four freedoms that have been couched in different language at different times but can be expressed as: freedom of speech and press, freedom of religion, freedom from fear, and freedom from want. The upright position of the bars signifies uprightness between men and uprightness between governments.

On April 25, 1945, representatives of forty-eight nations met for the United Nations Conference on International Organizations at San Francisco. There, in front of the Opera House, where the delegates convened, was flown the United Nations Flag, symbol of their consonant principles and their joint resolve.

INDEX